A YACHTSMAN'S GUIDE
TO THE
COLLISION
RULES

A YACHTSMAN'S GUIDE TO THE COLLISION RULES

The International Regulations
for Preventing Collisions at Sea
–explained

JOHN CAMPBELL

WATERLINE

First published in the UK in 1999
by Waterline Books, an imprint of Airlife Publishing Ltd

British Library Cataloguing-in-Publication Data
  A catalogue record for this book
  is available from the British Library

ISBN 1 84037 013 0

Printed in Italy

an imprint of Airlife Publishing Ltd
101 Longden Road, Shrewsbury, SY3 9EB, England
E-mail: airlife@airlifebooks.com

CONTENTS

Understanding the Collision Regulations.

INTRODUCTION

I had always learnt the Collision Regulations by rote, using one of the programmed learning guides. I found that I could learn the various disparate facts fairly quickly, certainly in time for any impending exam, but it seemed that I just as quickly forgot most of them after the exam.

When I was working for a commercial licence, the lecturers encouraged us not just to learn the Rules, but to understand them. Suddenly it all became clearer. As I began to understand the Rules, and their implications, I found that I had learnt them.

I usually find that once I fully understand something, then that knowledge is retained for a long time. If I simply learn a series of facts for an exam, that knowledge often fades rather quickly, as soon as the exam has been completed.

So whether you are needing to learn the Collision Regulations for an exam, or simply so you can sail safer, understanding the Rules will help you.

Each Rule is dealt with in a similar manner, using three type styles.

The Rule itself is highlighted in blue.
An explanation of each section of the Rule is then given, together with the implications of the Rule.
A summary of the Rule is given at the end.

If one is setting out to understand and learn the Rules, then it has been found best if each chapter is read in its entirety, including the quoted Rule, the explanation and the summary. The explanation and summary sections should then be read through two or three times more, to consolidate the knowledge. Finally, if you are working for an exam, go through the summaries another couple of times just before the exam. If you are simply learning the Rules for your own satisfaction, then concentrate on the explanation sections.

Do not try and do it all in one session. Work through a few Rules at a time, but do not cheat yourself by taking shortcuts. Take the time actually to read the Rule as written, as well as the explanation and the summary.

Also included are several mnemonics which I have used over the years to help remember various parts of the rules. Some of these I have made up myself, others I have 'borrowed' from friends. Perhaps you will be able to add some of your own.

Good luck, if you are working for an exam, and safe sailing.

SOUND SIGNALS

Signals when two vessels are in sight of one another

1. I am altering my course to starboard. — *one short blast (or flash)* — ●

2. I am altering my course to port. — *two short blasts (or flashes)* — ● ●

3. I am operating astern propulsion. — *three short blasts (or flashes)* — ● ● ●

4. I do not understand your intentions, or I disagree, or Wake Up. — *at least five short blasts (or flashes)* — ● ● ● ● ●

5. I intend to overtake you on your starboard side. — *two prolonged and a short blast* — ▬ ▬ ●

6. I intend to overtake you on your port side. — *two prolonged and two short blasts* — ▬ ▬ ● ●

7. I agree. — *prolonged, short, prolonged and short blasts (Morse code "C")* — ▬ ● ▬ ●

8. Approaching a blind bend or obstruction in a narrow channel. — *one prolonged blast* — ▬

Signals to be used in restricted visibility

1. Power-driven vessel making way, in restricted visibility. — *one prolonged blast, every two minutes or less* — ▬

2. Power-driven vessel underway, but stopped, in restricted visibility. — *two prolonged blasts, every two minutes or less* — ▬ ▬

3. Vessel not under command, restricted in ability to manoeuvre, constrained by draught, sailing vessel, vessel fishing, vessel towing or pushing another, vessel fishing at anchor, vessel restricted in ability to manoeuvre operating at anchor. — *one prolonged and two short blasts, every two minutes or less* — ▬ ● ●

4. Vessel being towed. — *one prolonged and three short blasts, every two minutes or less* — ▬ ● ● ●

5. Vessel at anchor, less than 100 metres in length. — *five seconds rapid ringing of bell every minute* — 🔔🔔🔔🔔🔔

6. Vessel at anchor, more than 100 metres in length. — *five seconds rapid ringing of bell, followed by five seconds rapid sounding of gong*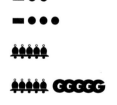

7. Optional whistle signal for vessel at anchor, in addition to bell and, if over 100 metres, gong signals. — *short, prolonged and short blasts on the whistle (Morse "R")* — ● ▬ ●

8. Vessel aground, less than 100 metres in length. — *three strokes on the bell, five seconds rapid ringing, then three more strokes on the bell* — 🔔🔔🔔 🔔🔔🔔🔔🔔 🔔🔔🔔

9. Vessel aground, more than 100 metres in length. — *three strokes on the bell, five seconds rapid ringing, then three more strokes on the bell, followed by five seconds rapid sounding of the gong*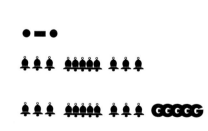

10. "Appropriate" whistle signal for vessel aground, in addition to bell, and, if over 100 metres, gong signals. — *Morse code "U"-you are standing into danger Two short and a prolonged blast* — ● ● ▬

11. Pilot vessel on duty, at anchor. — *five seconds rapid ringing of bell, followed by four short blasts on the whistle* — 🔔🔔🔔🔔🔔 ● ● ● ●

12. Pilot vessel on duty, making way. — *one prolonged blast every two minutes or less, followed by four short blasts*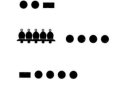

PART A.
GENERAL

Rule 1. Application

This rule tells us to whom, when and where the rules apply.

> a. These Rules shall apply to all vessels upon the high seas and in all waters connected therewith navigable by seagoing vessels.

The Rules apply to all vessels, regardless of size, and they apply not only on the high seas, but also on any waters connected to the high seas, that can be navigated by seagoing vessels. So ten miles up a river, the Rules still apply, just as they do in the middle of the Atlantic.

> b. Nothing in these Rules shall interfere with the operation of special rules made by an appropriate authority for roadsteads, harbours, rivers, lakes or inland waterways connected with the high seas and navigable by seagoing vessels. Such special rules shall conform as closely as possible to these Rules.

Coastal States retain the right to make special rules in roadsteads, rivers, lakes or inland waterways, even if they are connected with the sea and navigable by seagoing vessels. Many rivers, lakes and inland waterways do have their own rules particularly with respect to light and sound signals, but it should be remembered that such special rules can be extended to roadsteads, outside the normal limits of inland waterways. The existence of any such special rules can be found in the appropriate sailing directions.

The last part of the paragraph advises that any such special rules must follow the normal rules as closely as possible, so as not to cause confusion. For example, a Coastal State would be discouraged from having a special rule saying that in their waters all vessels must pass starboard-to-starboard instead of the normal port-to-port.

> c. Nothing in these Rules shall interfere with the operation of any special rules made by the Government of any State with respect to additional station or signal lights, shapes or whistle signals for ships of war and vessels proceeding under convoy, or with respect to additional station or signal lights or shapes for fishing vessels engaged in fishing as a fleet. These additional station or signal lights, shapes or whistle signals shall, so far as possible be such that they cannot be mistaken for any light, shape, or signal authorised elsewhere under these Rules.

Any State is allowed to authorise special lights, shapes and whistle signals for warships, vessels in convoy and for vessels fishing in a fleet, so long as the signals are such that they cannot be mistaken for, or confused with signals authorised under the Rules. Note that **Annex II** of the Rules stipulates special signals for trawlers and purse seine fishing boats, which have been accepted under international agreement.

> d. Traffic separation schemes may be adopted by the Organisation for the purpose of these Rules.

The Organisation referred to is the International Maritime Organisation, the **IMO**. **Rule 10** covers the operation of vessels within IMO recognised traffic separation schemes, and this part of **Rule 1** says that the IMO may adopt any scheme developed by a Coastal State for separating traffic into lanes. When such a scheme is adopted by the IMO, its existence will be included in the IMO publication "Ships' Routing", and **Rule 10** will be applicable to vessels using the scheme.

If a scheme has not been adopted by the IMO, then **Rule 10** does not apply, but common sense, and **Rule 2**, tell us that we should follow any suggested separation scheme as a matter of good seamanship.

> e. Whenever the Government concerned shall have determined that a vessel of special construction or purpose cannot comply fully with the provisions of any of these Rules with respect to the number, position,

> range or arc of visibility of lights or shapes, as well as to the disposition and characteristics of sound-signalling appliances, such vessel shall comply with such other provisions in regard to the number, position, range or arc of visibility of lights or shapes, as well as to the disposition and characteristics of sound-signalling appliances, as her Government shall have determined to be the closest possible compliance with these Rules in respect of that vessel.

A Flag State, that is a country under whose flag a vessel is registered, is allowed to exempt particular vessels from compliance with all of the requirements for lights and/or sound-signalling apparatus, if the construction of the vessel makes it difficult to comply.

Warships often find it difficult to comply. For example, aircraft carriers are allowed to have their masthead lights offset, because having masts on the centreline would interfere with the operation of aircraft. Submarines will show two masthead lights, but, in contravention of Annex I, the forward one may be lower than the sidelights, which are usually mounted on the conning tower.

When the Rules changed from imperial measurements to metric, many vessels were faced with moving lights a short distance, just to comply with the new metric measurements. We will see in **Rule 38** that a nine year exemption was granted, to allow time for the lights to be moved, but this part of the Rule allows a Flag State to give permanent exemption to the positioning of one or more lights.

The last part of this inordinately long sentence says that if dispensation is granted for one light or shape, then the vessel must, as far as possible, comply with all the other requirements. So while the aircraft carrier is allowed to have offset masthead lights, it must comply with the requirements for the arcs of visibility of all the lights, and the positioning of sidelights and stern light.

Summary of Rule 1. Application.

1. *These Rules apply to all vessels, on the high seas and on all waters connected to the high seas which are navigable by seagoing vessels.*
2. *Coastal States can make their own rules in their own waters, but they should follow these International Rules as closely as possible.*
3. *Flag States can make their own Rules as to special lights, shapes and sound signals for their own vessels, particularly warships and fishing vessels, but these must be such that they cannot be mistaken for signals in these Rules.*
4. *Flag States can grant dispensation to any of their vessels which cannot comply with all the requirements of lights, shapes or sound signalling apparatus.*
5. *The International Maritime Organisation may choose to*

adopt a locally implemented traffic separation scheme, at which time Rule 10 will be enforced within the scheme. Common sense, and Rule 2 suggest that we should comply with the recommendations of any traffic separation scheme, even if it is not recognised by the IMO.

Rule 2. Responsibility

This is sometimes termed the Seamanship Rule.

> a.   Nothing in these Rules shall exonerate any vessel, or the owner, master or crew thereof, from the consequences of any neglect to comply with these Rules or of the neglect of any precaution which may be required by the ordinary practice of seamen, or by the special circumstances of the case.

We cannot blame the Rules if we have a collision, common sense, and good seamanship must prevail.

For example, in **Rule 1.d.** we saw that a local Traffic Separation Scheme could be adopted by the IMO, at which time compliance with the scheme would become compulsory under international law, and **Rule 10** would apply to vessels using the scheme. Until such time as the scheme is adopted by the IMO, then theoretically under **Rules 1 and 10**, vessels legally would not have to follow the routes through the traffic scheme. Obviously this would be dangerous, and **Rule 2 a.** is telling us that we should not, indeed must not, rigidly follow the Rules to the exclusion of good seamanship. Good seamanship tells us that we should follow the lanes in a traffic separation scheme, even if it is not an IMO approved one.

> b.   In construing and complying with these Rules due regard shall be had to all dangers of navigation and collision and to any special circumstances, including the limitations of the vessels involved, which may make a departure from these Rules necessary to avoid immediate danger.

This again is telling us that good seamanship should prevail. It is saying that we not only can, but must deviate from the Rules to avoid a collision if there are special circumstances, or if the other vessel is having difficulty manoeuvring. An example of this would be if two vessels are approaching each other in a river. It is much easier for the vessel that is motoring against the current to manoeuvre than the vessel that is travelling with the current. The vessel going up-stream can slow down and stem the current, yet still retain control, so good seamanship suggests that this vessel should keep clear of the vessel which is travelling with the current, even if she would otherwise have right of way under the rules.

Likewise, a small sailing vessel should not expect a super-tanker to be able to able to alter course rapidly to avoid a collision. The sailing vessel, or indeed any small vessel should be navigated in such a way as to avoid a close quarters situation developing with a much larger vessel.

Although **Rule 2** tells us we can and must deviate from the Rules if necessary to avoid a collision, it does not allow us to do so as a matter of convenience, only when it is necessary. We must not cross somebody's bows and try to pass them starboard-to-starboard, just because it would save us some distance. We must follow the Rules, and pass them port-to-port, and only alter course once we are past and clear.

Summary of Rule 2. Responsibility
(The Seamanship Rule).

1. *You cannot blame the Rules if you have a collision.*
2. *You can, and must, deviate from the Rules if necessary to avoid a collision, and good seamanship must prevail over rigidly following the Rules.*
3. *You cannot deviate from the Rules as a matter of convenience, only from necessity to avoid a risk of collision.*

Rule 3. General Definitions

This Rule defines many of the terms used in the Rules. Many of them are fairly obvious, but there are some subtleties worth noting.

> For the purpose of these Rules, except where the context otherwise requires:
> a. The word "vessel" includes every description of water craft, including non-displacement craft and seaplanes, used or capable of being used as a means of transportation on water.

Even the smallest craft capable of carrying a person on the water is to be considered as a vessel, so a windsurfer is a vessel for the purposes of the Rules, and is expected to observe the Rules in the same way as any other vessel.

Hydrofoils and hovercraft are non-displacement craft. This section of **Rule 3** makes it plain that a hovercraft is to be considered as a vessel, not an aircraft.

A seaplane too, when it is on the water, is a vessel. When we get to **Rule 18**, we will see that a seaplane, while it is on the water, is required to keep clear of all other vessels, but in every other respect, it is to be considered in the same way as any other vessel.

> b. The term "power-driven vessel" means any vessel propelled by machinery.

A dinghy with an outboard motor is a power-driven vessel, and as we shall see in **Section C.**, so is a sailing vessel if it has its engine running, and engaged in gear.

There is an anomaly here which the Rule-makers seem to have missed. **Rule 23** states that all "power-driven vessels", when underway, shall exhibit masthead lights, yet when we get to **Rule 26** we shall find that "vessels engaged in fishing other than trawling" do not, and under **Rule 27**, neither do vessels "not under command", even if making way. Also **Rule 18**, Responsibilities Between Vessels, differentiates between power-driven vessels, vessels not under command, vessels restricted in their ability to manoeuvre, and fishing vessels. So at risk of being slightly pedantic, **Rule 3.b** is not, strictly speaking, true – vessels not under command, vessels restricted in their ability to manoeuvre and fishing vessels should be excluded, and not classed as "power-driven vessels" for the purposes of the Rules.

> c. The term "sailing vessel" means any vessel under sail provided that propelling machinery, if fitted, is not being used.

A sailing vessel loses its privileges as soon as the engine is used to assist propulsion. From that moment it becomes a power-driven vessel, even if all the sails are still set.

We will see that part of **Rule 25** says that such a vessel must indicate that it is a power-driven vessel, by hoisting a cone, point down, in the forward rigging.

> d. The term "vessel engaged in fishing" means any vessel fishing with nets, lines, trawls or other fishing apparatus which restrict manoeuvrability, but does not include a vessel fishing with trolling lines or other fishing apparatus which do not restrict manoeuvrability.

We are not allowed to put a fishing line out of the back of the boat and call ourselves a fishing vessel, to claim extra privileges. The privileges are only granted to those vessels which are hampered by their gear. So a fishing boat on her way out, or on her way back from the fishing grounds, if she does not have her gear out, is not classed as a fishing vessel. Such a vessel is accorded no special privileges, and should not show any of the signals which are applicable to fishing vessels, although lots of them do!

> e. The word "seaplane" includes any aircraft designed to manoeuvre on the water.

Any aircraft that is able to operate from the water is classed as a seaplane. A pilot will call an aircraft which can land only on water a seaplane, and one which can land on either water or the land, an amphibian. For the purposes of these Rules, they are all seaplanes.

> f.   The term "vessel not under command" means a vessel which through some exceptional circumstance is unable to manoeuvre as required by these Rules and is therefore unable to keep out of the way of another vessel.

The important words here are **exceptional circumstance**. A vessel cannot elect to be classed as not under command just for convenience sake. For example, if waiting to enter a harbour, a vessel is not allowed to heave-to, show the signals for not under command, and expect other vessels to keep clear, while the crew takes a nap. Such a vessel must maintain a watch, keep her engines ready to manoeuvre, and avoid other vessels if required.

Similarly, a yacht sailing short-handed is not justified in showing the signals for not under command, just because the crew elect not to keep a watch. In this situation, there is no exceptional circumstance – the crew of the yacht chose to go to sea short-handed.

Bad weather, if it is truly exceptional in relation to the size and capabilities of the vessel concerned, may possibly be classed as an exceptional circumstance, but only if such weather seriously affects the ability of the vessel to manoeuvre. Under such conditions the vessel may be justified in showing the signals for not under command.

More usual circumstances for a vessel to be classed as not under command include breakdown of engines, breakdown of steering gear, anchors down but not holding, or a sailing vessel becalmed, provided she does not have an auxiliary engine available.

It should be remembered that the signal for not under command is not a distress signal, and the vessel is not asking for assistance – she is only asking that you keep clear.

> g.   The term "vessel restricted in her ability to manoeuvre" means a vessel which from the nature of her work is restricted in her ability to manoeuvre as required by these Rules and is therefore unable to keep out of the way of another vessel.
>
> The term "vessels restricted in their ability to manoeuvre" shall include but not be limited to:
> i.   a vessel engaged in laying, servicing or picking up a navigation mark, submarine cable or pipeline;
> ii.   a vessel engaged in dredging, surveying or underwater operations;
> iii. a vessel engaged in replenishment or transferring persons, provisions or cargo while underway;
> iv.   a vessel engaged in the launching or recovery of aircraft;
> v.   a vessel engaged in mine clearance operations;
> vi.   a vessel engaged in a towing operation such as severely restricts the towing vessel and her tow in their ability to deviate from their course.

As it says in the lead-in to the list, this list is not meant to be complete. Any vessel which is doing a job that limits its ability to manoeuvre in accordance with the Rules is classed as a "vessel restricted in her ability to manoeuvre". We shall see that such a vessel is obliged to show certain signals, and is to be granted certain privileges as to right of way.

It should be noted that a tug with a "normal" tow is not classed as restricted in her ability to manoeuvre, and is accorded no special privileges. She is classed as a power-driven vessel, and treated accordingly under the Rules.

> h.   The term "vessel constrained by her draught" means a power-driven vessel which because of her draught in relation to the available depth and width of navigable water is severely restricted in her ability to deviate from the course she is following.

We will see that a vessel which is classed as constrained by her draught is required to show particular signals, and is granted certain privileges as to right of way.

The most important point of this definition is the fact that it is not only the depth, but the width of the navigable water that is to be considered. A vessel drawing 5 metres in a channel 6 metres deep, would not be considered to be constrained by her draught if the channel was a mile or two wide. However, the same vessel, drawing 5 metres in a channel 10 metres deep could be considered to be constrained by her draught, if the channel was very narrow, and the surrounding water was perhaps only 4 metres deep. It is the width of the available channel that is more important than the actual under-keel clearance.

The definition stipulates that the constrained vessel must be a power-driven vessel, so sailing vessels cannot consider themselves to be constrained by their draught. When we get to **Rule 18**, we will see that a sailing vessel must avoid impeding the safe passage of a vessel constrained by her draught. If the depth and width of navigable water is limiting the ability of a sailing vessel to avoid impeding a vessel which is showing the signals that it is constrained by its draught, then the sailing vessel should consider starting the engine, if it has one, and becoming a power-driven vessel. If it has no engine, then perhaps it should be seeking a tow, or anchoring until it is safe to proceed.

> i.   The word "underway" means that a vessel is not at anchor, nor made fast to the shore, nor aground.

We must differentiate between *underway* and *making way*.

This part of the Rule says that a vessel is *underway* whenever it is not secured to the ground, either by means of an anchor, by lines to the shore or by being aground. *Making way* means that the vessel is actually moving through the water. A vessel can be underway but stopped in the water, and so she would not be making way. For example a vessel may be stopped in the water, perhaps waiting for a tide to rise sufficiently for her to enter a harbour. She is not moving through the water, so she is not *making way*, but as long as she **is not at anchor, made fast to the shore, or aground**, she is still considered to be *underway*. As such, she must still keep a lookout (Rule 5), and have her engines ready to manoeuvre, to keep out of the way of other vessels if necessary.

A vessel with her anchor down, but dragging, is considered to be underway. She may be classed as not under command, but she is still underway, and if she is moving through the water, she would of course be considered to be making way.

We will find several of the Rules stipulate different light and sound signals for vessels underway but stopped, and for vessels making way.

> j.   The words "length" and "breadth" of a vessel mean her length overall and greatest breadth.

There are many lengths associated with a vessel, and this part of the Rule stipulates that it is the length overall that applies. LOA is measured from the foremost point to the aftermost point of the vessel – this will probably not be the same as the length shown on the certificate of registry, which is usually the length from the stem to the rudder post.

> k.   Vessels shall be deemed to be in sight of one another only when one can be observed visually from the other.

This definition is particularly important when we consider **Rule 19 – Restricted Visibility**. It does not matter if two vessels can "see" each other on the radar, if they cannot be seen visually by each other then they are not deemed to be in sight of each other, and we will see that **Rule 19** applies. However, if subsequently they get close enough to sight each other visually, then **Rule 19** ceases to apply, and the "visual" Rules **(Rules 12 to 18)** come into effect.

A vessel cannot claim that another vessel was not in sight just because a poor lookout was being kept. If it is *possible* to see one vessel from the other, even if it necessitates the use of binoculars, then it is deemed to be in sight.

> l.   The term "restricted visibility" means any condition in which visibility is restricted by fog, mist, falling snow, heavy rainstorms, sandstorms or any other similar causes.

It does not have to be thick fog for the visibility to be "restricted". Any time that the visibility is reduced for any reason, the visibility is deemed to be restricted. If a heat-haze reduces the visibility to say five miles, the visibility could be deemed to be restricted. Other things which could restrict visibility include smoke and dust, as well as fog, mist, snow, rain and blowing sand as stipulated in the Rule.

Rule 6, the Safe Speed Rule refers to visibility, and **Rule 19** deals specifically with restricted visibility, when vessels are not in sight of each other.

Summary Rule 3. Definitions.

1. *Anything capable of carrying people on the water is classed as a* **vessel**, *including hovercraft, hydrofoils, and while they are on the water, seaplanes.*

2. *A* **sailing vessel** *which has an engine contributing to the propulsion is classed as a power-driven vessel.*

3. *A vessel can only consider itself* **not under command** *if some <u>exceptional circumstance</u> has rendered the vessel unable to manoeuvre.*

4. *A vessel* **Restricted in her Ability to Manoeuvre** *is limited in her ability to manoeuvre by the nature of her work. This includes vessels:*
   * *working on pipelines, cables or navigation marks;*
   * *dredging, surveying or diving operations;*
   * *transferring people, provisions or cargo between vessels underway;*
   * *launching or recovering aircraft;*
   * *mine-sweeping – minesweepers show their own special signals;*
   * *towing, if the tow is such that it makes it difficult for the tug to alter course. A normal tow does not warrant a vessel considering itself as restricted in its ability to manoeuvre, nor does a "normal" tow grant any special privileges to the towing vessel.*

5. *A vessel* **constrained by her draught** *must be a power-driven vessel. She is restricted in her navigation by the <u>width</u> of the navigable channel.*

6. **Underway** *means not at anchor, aground nor made fast to the shore. A vessel moving through the water is* **making way**.

7. *Vessels are deemed to be* **in sight** *of one another when they can see each other visually as opposed to detecting each other only by radar.*

8. **Restricted visibility** *means any time the visibility is reduced. It includes fog, mist, rain, snow, sandstorms, dust and smoke.*

Part B.
STEERING AND SAILING RULES
SECTION ONE: Conduct of Vessels in any Condition of Visibility

The Steering and Sailing Rules are divided into three sections:

1. Conduct of vessels in any condition of visibility - Rules 4-10
2. Conduct of vessels in sight of one another - Rules 11-18
3. Conduct of vessels in restricted visibility - Rule 19

Rule 4. Application

> Rules in this section apply in any condition of visibility.

This Rule states that the Rules in this section, i.e. **Rules 5 to 10**, apply in all conditions of visibility. They apply regardless of whether or not other vessels are in sight. They apply <u>at all times</u>.

Summary Rule 4. Application.

Rules in Section B. I., (i.e. Rules 5 to 10) apply to all vessels, at all times, and in all states of visibility.

Rule 5. Look-out

> Every vessel shall at all times maintain a proper look-out by sight and hearing as well as by all available means appropriate in the prevailing circumstances and conditions so as to make a full appraisal of the situation and of the risk of collision.

This is the most important of all the Rules. If you are ever asked by an examiner which is the most important Rule, he wants to hear "Rule 5". If you do not keep a look-out, you cannot avoid any potential collisions. Let's look at the Rule in detail:

It says we must keep a look-out at all times. As far as the Rule is concerned, it is not good enough to look around every ten minutes or so, we are supposed to be keeping a look-out <u>at all times</u>.

We are not supposed to be just looking, but listening as well. In clear weather, the listening part of the watch is probably more concerned with the radio, listening for distress signals or navigational warnings. However, in restricted visibility, it is important to keep a listening watch for fog signals, and this cannot be done from inside a wheelhouse with the door shut!

In restricted visibility there should be a lookout placed as far forward in the vessel as it is safe to do. They should not only be looking, but listening as well, even if the vessel has radar operating.

This Rule is also telling us that we must use "all available means", and several courts have said that this includes the use of radar, if it is fitted. So if we have radar on board, we are actually legally obliged to use it.

The Rule finishes off by saying that we must "make a full appraisal of the situation and risk of collision." If the visual look-out is our primary look-out, then when we sight another vessel, we should take a compass bearing of that vessel. If the compass bearing stays steady, then there is a risk of collision, and we should be prepared to act accordingly.

If a vessel is detected by radar, then it must be systematically plotted to determine if there is a risk of collision. To do such a plot is not only helpful in determining if there is a risk of collision, and what action to take, but when we get to Rule 7 – Risk of collision, we will see that it is actually obligatory to plot radar targets.

The most rudimentary form of plot is a series of bearings – again if the bearing remains constant, then there is a risk of collision, but a proper plot of an approaching vessel will give us much more information. It will not only show how close it will pass, but it will also indicate the true heading of the vessel and its aspect. This knowledge will help us to take the correct action in avoiding any possible collision. (An appendix on basic radar plotting techniques is included after the Rules.)

The duty of the look-out is to report any vessel, light, floating object or land that is sighted, and in the case of restricted visibility, any fog signals heard. However, in a busy area it would be impossible to report each and every sighting, so look-outs should be able to use their judgement, and report only those vessels, lights or objects which present a possible risk of collision, or might serve as an aid to navigation.

Summary of Rule 5. Look-out.

1. *Every vessel must keep a lookout at all times, by sight, hearing and all available means, which is generally accepted to include the use of radar, even in conditions of good visibility.*
2. *There is a duty to make a full appraisal of the situation and risk of collision. For vessels sighted visually, bearings should be taken, and for those detected by radar, a plot should be made of the other vessel, so the risk of collision can be assessed. (See also Rule 7 – Risk of Collision.)*

Rule 6. Safe Speed (Rule Six is Safe Speed)

> Every vessel shall at all times proceed at a safe speed so that she can take proper and effective action to avoid collision and be stopped within a distance appropriate to the prevailing circumstances and conditions.

All vessels must proceed at a safe speed **at all times**, so the watchkeeper must continuously monitor and appraise the conditions, and be aware of any change in visibility, and be prepared to reduce speed immediately if conditions change.

The term **safe speed** is rather subjective. If a vessel is involved in a collision, it does not necessarily follow that she was going too fast. Indeed, it could be that she was going too slowly to be able to manoeuvre effectively, especially if she were trying to manoeuvre in a strong current, or in a strong wind.

In open ocean, a particular speed might be considered safe for a given visibility, whereas in coastal waters, in heavy traffic, for the same visibility, that speed could well be considered too fast.

The next part of the Rule specifies some of the factors that we must consider in deciding what is a safe speed for any particular condition.

> In determining a safe speed the following factors shall be among those taken into account:
> a. By all vessels:
>   i.   the state of visibility;
>   ii. the traffic density including concentrations of fishing vessels or any other vessels;
>   iii. the manoeuvrability of the vessel with special reference to stopping distance and turning ability in the prevailing conditions;
>   iv. at night the presence of background light such as from shore lights or from back scatter of her own lights;
>   v.   the state of wind, sea and current, and the proximity of navigational hazards;
>   vi. the draught in relation to the available depth of water.
>
> b. Additionally, by vessels with operational radar:
>   i.   the characteristics, efficiency and limitations of the radar equipment;
>   ii. any constraints imposed by the radar range scale in use;
>   iii. the effect on radar detection of the sea state, weather and other sources of interference;
>   iv. the possibility that small vessels, ice and other floating objects may not be detected by radar at an adequate range;

> v. the number, location and movement of vessels detected by radar;
> vi. the more exact assessment of the visibility that may be possible when radar is used to determine the range of vessels or other objects in the vicinity.

Let's look at the six points which are applicable to all vessels:

i. **Visibility**. A safe speed is often taken as the speed at which a vessel can stop within half the distance of the visibility. The thinking being that if two vessels are approaching each other, and each can stop within half the distance when they sight each other, then there should not be a risk of collision. However, this allows no time for either helmsman to assess the situation, before taking action.

For example, a high speed vessel would probably not be justified in making twenty-five knots, in visibility of say half a mile, even if it were capable of making an emergency stop within less than a quarter of a mile. At that speed, in such visibility there would be little, or no time to assess the risk of collision if another vessel were sighted. A safe speed will often be slower than that required to stop in half the distance of visibility.

Conversely, a vessel in mid-ocean, where there was little chance of meeting small vessels, would not be expected to stop if she encountered visibility of say 50 metres, particularly if she had radar which was being properly used. But neither would she be justified in travelling at twenty knots.

The range of visibility must be monitored and continuously assessed. This is especially true at night, when a decrease in visibility can often go unnoticed.

Determining a safe speed for a particular visibility comes down to a question of judgement and good seamanship.

ii. **Density of traffic**. If there are many vessels in the vicinity, particularly lots of fishing boats which have privileges over power-driven vessels, then obviously a safe speed is slower than if there were few or no other vessels in the area.

iii. **Manoeuvrability and stopping distance**. A high degree of manoeuvrability and good stopping ability still does not justify excessive speed in restricted visibility. The vessel may be justified in going faster than a less manoeuvrable vessel, but the speed must be slow enough to allow time for assessment of the situation, so **proper and effective action** can be taken **to avoid collision**.

iv. **Lights and back scatter**. Shore lights, and the back scatter from one's own lights, while not reducing the range of visibility as such, can make it much more difficult to see the lights of other vessels, and indeed lights of navigational aids. Under such conditions, a safe speed will be lower than if there were no interfering lights.

v. **Wind, weather and navigational hazards**. Running before an on-shore gale, towards a narrow channel on a lee-shore, warrants a slower speed of approach. There is probably little room for error, and limited scope for manoeuvre if another vessel is encountered. A slow speed will give more time for assessment.

Although the Rules are primarily concerned with preventing collisions between vessels, if there is a navigational hazard nearby, perhaps an unmarked rock or reef, then good seamanship suggests that speed should be further reduced. Once more, a slower speed gives extra time to check the navigation, but also, if there is a possibility of hitting something, it is better to do it at a slower rather than faster speed!

vi. **Draught**. Many vessels are more difficult to manoeuvre in shallow water than in deeper water. Obviously what is perceived as shallow depends on the draught of the vessel. What we are really concerned with is what is termed "under-keel clearance." The effects of a small under-keel clearance on the manoeuvrability of a vessel are much reduced at lower speeds. Also, at small under-keel clearances there is an increased possibility of hitting some obstruction on the sea-bed, and as before, if there is a chance of hitting something it is better to be going slowly.

The draught of the vessel may limit it to a relatively narrow channel, which could make it more difficult to avoid a collision or a close quarters situation. In such cases, once more, speed should be reduced.

Now we will look at the six points to be considered by vessels fitted with radar:

i. **Efficiency**. The use of a modern radar set fitted with ARPA (**A**utomatic **R**adar **P**lotting **A**id), which is capable of plotting perhaps as many as twenty or thirty targets at the same time, might possibly justify a higher speed under certain conditions than in the case of a vessel using a radar that requires manual plotting of all the targets.

ii. **Range Scale**. Consideration must always be given to the range scale in use on the radar. If the radar is being operated on a short range, perhaps because it is being used to locate a nearby navigational mark, then it cannot be used for plotting distant, but approaching vessels, to assess any risk of collision. Conversely, if the radar is being used on a long range, perhaps to plot a distant vessel or locate a harbour entrance, then the definition and discrimination of the radar signal could be such that nearby targets are missed altogether.

The correct way to use the radar is to change ranges regularly, so both near and distant targets can be detected and plotted, but there may be times when a particular range must be used for a period of time, such as when searching for a distant navigation mark. Under such circumstances, it may be prudent to slow down to allow more time to assess the situation, and to search for targets on other ranges.

iii. **Sea, weather and other interference**. Interference caused by waves or by rain is termed "clutter." The radar set will have controls for reducing the effect of sea clutter and rain clutter, but great care must be taken to use these controls correctly, otherwise weak targets will be suppressed along with the interference. 10 cm radar is less affected by clutter than is 3 cm radar. If a vessel has two radar sets, one of each type, then she would be expected to use the 10 cm radar for detecting targets in areas of clutter, such as approaching rain squalls. The watch-keeper must be aware of the limitations of the radar to detect targets in areas of clutter, and speed should be reduced before entering such an area, or indeed, even before passing close by such an area.

iv. **Small vessels and ice**. Small vessels, particularly those built of wood or reinforced plastic, will often give a very poor radar return, unless they are fitted with an effective radar reflector. If passing through an area where small fishing boats could be operating, or coastal areas where there might be small yachts, then speed should be reduced, so the vessel can be stopped within half the range of the visibility, or less. In oceanic waters, there is less likelihood of meeting such vessels, and any that do venture far from shore are more likely to be equipped with a radar reflector, so a higher speed might be justified.

Ice is notoriously bad at returning a reliable echo. Even quite large icebergs will often remain invisible to the radar, and smaller pieces, floating low in the water will almost never appear on the radar, even though they are large enough to damage most vessels. If the vessel is operating in an area where there is a possibility of ice, then speed should be reduced so that the vessel can be stopped within the range of the visibility, and an additional visual lookout posted.

v. **Movement of other vessels**. If there are several other vessels detected by the radar to be in the vicinity, and some of them are likely to cause a close quarters situation, then again, speed should be reduced. This is not necessarily to lessen damage in any possible collision, but to allow more time to assess the situation by plotting the targets, and to take action to avoid a close quarters situation developing.

Vessels approaching from ahead, or nearly ahead, present the greatest risk and allow the least time for assessment before action must be taken. Overtaking vessels will generally be closing at a relatively slower speed.

However, when travelling in a traffic separation scheme, it may not be wise to slow down too much, if this results in lots of other vessels trying to overtake. It is better, as far as possible to keep the same speed as the majority of vessels in the traffic lane, but doing this cannot justify excessive speed. There has to be a happy medium. When in a traffic lane, particular watch should be kept for crossing traffic, and when we get to **Rule 10**, we shall see that being in a traffic lane does not give us any special right of way over crossing vessels. Except for situations with vessels of less than 20 metres, sailing vessels or fishing vessels crossing a traffic lane, normal sailing rules apply.

vi. **Visibility**. A vessel equipped with radar can measure the visibility, by watching when another vessel or navigation mark can first be seen visually, or when it disappears. The radar can then be used to measure the range of the target at that moment, which is the current visibility. This can be particularly useful at night, when a decrease in visibility is often hard to detect. If a radar target is showing just a few miles away, yet no lights are visible, rather than assuming it is an unlit vessel or object, consider the possibility that the visibility has decreased, and if necessary, slow down.

Summary Rule 6. Safe Speed. (Six is Safe Speed)

1. Every vessel shall at all times proceed at a safe speed so she can take proper and effective action to avoid collision.

2. The six factors to be taken into consideration by all vessels are:
   Visibility
   Density (of traffic)
   Manoeuvrability (of own vessel)
   Lights (shore lights and back scatter)
   Wind and weather, and proximity of hazards
   Draught.
   When I had to learn these for an exam, I made up a little mnemonic to remind me of the first letter of each key word. My mnemonic is:
Very Dry Martinis Lay Willy Down. Maybe you can think of a better one!

3. The six additional factors to be taken into consideration by vessels with radar are:
   Efficiency and limitations of radar
   Range in use, and any constraints
   Sea and rain clutter, or any other interference
   Small vessels and ice may not show
   Movement and number of vessels shown on radar
   Visibility – can make a more accurate assessment using the radar.

   For what it is worth, my mnemonic for these six is:
Every Radar Sees Small Motor Vessels. Although this is not strictly true, it helps me remember the six factors!

Rule 7. Risk of Collision

> a. Every vessel shall use all available means appropriate to the prevailing circumstances and conditions to determine if risk of collision exists. If there is any doubt such risk shall be deemed to exist.

The word **shall** means that it is compulsory to **use all available means** to determine if there is a risk of collision. **All available means** has been taken by many courts to include the use of radar, and just in case there is any doubt, the next paragraph spells it out for us.

> b. Proper use shall be made of radar equipment if fitted and operational, including long-range scanning to obtain early warning of risk of collision and radar plotting or equivalent systematic observation of detected objects.

Once again, **shall** means that it is compulsory to use the radar if it is fitted, not just if we feel like it, or if the visibility is bad. It is also saying that **proper use** shall be made of the radar. Just in case there is any doubt as to what constitutes **proper use**, it explains it for us – we have to use a long range to scan for approaching targets, and we must plot the targets in some way, so we can determine if there is a risk of collision developing.

> c. Assumptions shall not be made on the basis of scanty information, especially scanty radar information.

With this paragraph they are telling us that when we detect another vessel by the radar, we must not alter course, nor indeed stand on, without having a clear understanding of the situation. The only way to get such an understanding is to do a systematic plot of the other vessel, and so determine if it will present a risk of collision. We must not make assumptions as to what the other vessel is doing. We must gather sufficient information so that we know what it is doing, and then take whatever action is necessary.

> d. In determining if risk of collision exists the following considerations shall be among those taken into account :
> i. such risk shall be deemed to exist if the compass bearing of an approaching vessel does not appreciably change;
> ii. such risk may sometimes exist even when an appreciable bearing change is evident, particularly when approaching a very large vessel or a tow or when approaching a vessel at close range.

The easiest way to determine if there is a risk of collision is to take a series of compass bearings of the other vessel. If the bearing stays the same, or shows very little change, then there is a risk of collision. Such compass bearings can be taken visually, using a hand-bearing compass or an azimuth ring on the steering compass, or they can be taken using the radar.

Taking radar bearings is much easier if the radar is compass stabilised. If the radar is not interfaced to a gyro or to a fluxgate compass, then the bearings must be taken with reference to the ship's heading. When using an un-stabilised radar, which will be showing "ship's head up", it is more accurate to convert a series of relative bearings to compass bearings, by referring to the ship's heading at the instant when each bearing is taken, rather just relying on the relative bearings themselves. If only the relative bearings are used, then an unnoticed alteration of the course of one's own vessel could suggest that the bearing of the approaching vessel is changing, when in fact it is constant.

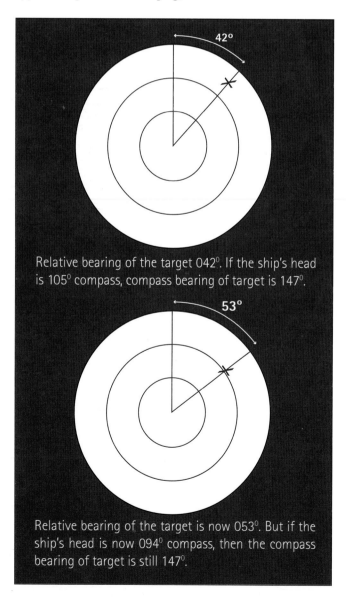

Relative bearing of the target 042°. If the ship's head is 105° compass, compass bearing of target is 147°.

Relative bearing of the target is now 053°. But if the ship's head is now 094° compass, then the compass bearing of target is still 147°.

Figure 7.1 Relative bearings of a radar target converted to compass bearings.

Likewise, taking bearings of an approaching ship by sighting across some structure on board your vessel is not a very reliable method. Any alteration of your own vessel's course, or slight movement of the observer's position could suggest that the bearing of an approaching vessel is changing, when in fact it could again be constant.

The second sub-paragraph of this rule warns us that a changing bearing does not guarantee that there is not risk of collision. You could be taking bearings of the bows of a large approaching vessel, and this bearing could be changing quite rapidly at close quarters, but you could still hit the stern of the vessel, or vice versa. Particularly when taking bearings of a large vessel, take the bearings of the part of the vessel that will pass closest to you. If you think the other vessel will be passing ahead of you, then take bearings of his stern.

The Rule also warns us of the danger of taking bearings of an approaching tug, and forgetting about its tow. The bearing of the tug could be changing quite rapidly, but had we been taking bearings of the tow, those could well have been constant, warning us of a risk of collision with the tow. Never pass astern of a tug, until you have identified any tow that he might have behind him, and have assessed any possible risk of collision with it.

There is a third scenario, which we are not specifically warned about. If we are approaching another vessel which is making a series of small course alterations, we could observe a significant change in the bearing of the other vessel, yet still find there is a risk of collision. We shall see that when we get to **Rule 8**, we are told we must make large alterations of course rather than a series of small alterations. One of the reasons for this, is to avoid exactly this situation.

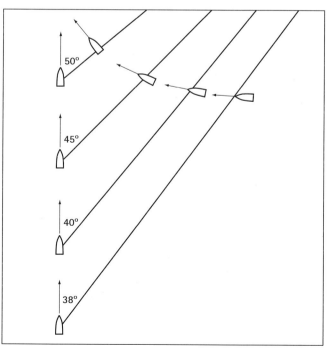

Figure 7.2. Approaching another vessel which is making a series of course alterations. The bearing of the other ship is changing, but there is still a risk of collision.

Summary of Rule 7. Risk of Collision.

1. *We must use all available means to determine if a risk of collision exists. This includes radar. If the vessel is fitted with radar, then it is compulsory to use it.*

2. *Radar must be used "properly", and this includes using it on a long range to get early warning of a risk of collision, and to plot targets systematically, to determine what they are doing, rather than to make assumptions.*

3. *A constant compass bearing of an approaching vessel suggests that there is a risk of collision, but a changing bearing does not guarantee that there is not.*
   - *A big vessel at close quarters can have a changing bearing of part of its structure, yet still present a risk of collision.*
   - *A tug may have a changing bearing, but its tow could offer a risk of collision.*
   - *An approaching vessel which is making a series of small alterations of course can have a changing bearing, but still present a risk of collision.*

Rule 8. Action to Avoid Collision

> a. Any action taken to avoid collision shall, if the circumstances of the case admit, be positive, made in ample time and with due regard to the observance of good seamanship.

Wherever possible, any action taken to avoid a collision must be **positive**, that is, one which leaves no doubt as to the vessel's intentions. Such action should also be taken in **ample time**, so that the navigator does not have to make hasty decisions at the last minute. Remember that **Rule 7. c.** – Risk of Collision, told us that we must not make decisions on the basis of scanty information, especially on the basis of scanty radar information. If the developing situation is being properly monitored, then there should be **ample time** to assess the situation, and act accordingly.

The navigator must, as always, exercise **good seamanship**. For example, he should make sure that there is not a vessel about to overtake him, before suddenly altering course to avoid a risk of collision with another vessel.

When we get to **Rule 34**, we shall see that we must make the appropriate whistle signal before altering course to avoid a risk of collision with another vessel, if we are in sight of that vessel.

> b. Any alteration of course and/or speed to avoid collision shall, if the circumstances of the case admit, be large enough to be readily apparent to another vessel observing visually or by radar; a succession of small alterations of course and/or speed should be avoided.

An alteration of course of 10° is unlikely to be readily apparent to another vessel, whether it is observing your vessel visually or by radar. An alteration of about 30° should be regarded as a minimum, and 60° to 90° would be preferable. Such an alteration should be readily apparent to an observer, and leave him in no doubt as to your intentions. Many collisions have been caused by one or both vessels making a series of small alterations in course or speed. Under such circumstances, the bearing of one vessel from the other may be changing, yet they could still be on a collision course.

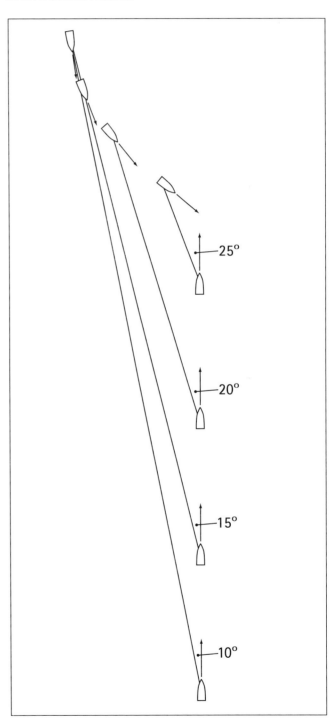

Fig 8.1. Give-way vessel making a series of small course alterations resulting in a collision situation even though the bearing from the stand-on vessel is changing.

In a crossing situation, the vessel which is giving way, i.e. the vessel which has the other on her starboard bow, should alter course sufficiently to put the other vessel on the port bow. At night this would allow the port navigation light to be seen, and by day would show an obvious change of aspect of the vessel. Once the intentions of the give-way vessel are apparent to the stand-on vessel, then it can slowly come back on to its original course, as the stand-on vessel passes.

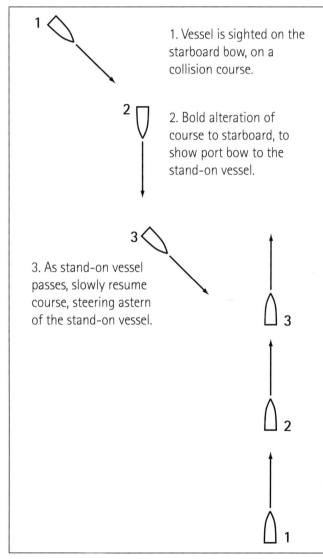

1. Vessel is sighted on the starboard bow, on a collision course.

2. Bold alteration of course to starboard, to show port bow to the stand-on vessel.

3. As stand-on vessel passes, slowly resume course, steering astern of the stand-on vessel.

Figure 8.2. The correct action by the give-way vessel is to make a large alteration to starboard, to show its port navigation light to the stand-on vessel. As the stand-on vessel passes, the give-way vessel can slowly return to her course. This way, the stand-on vessel is never in doubt as to the intentions of the give-way vessel.

An alteration of speed will generally take much longer to be effective, and also longer to become apparent to the other vessel. A slight reduction of speed should be avoided, as this may not be noticed by the other vessel. If you choose to slow down to avoid another vessel, then slow to half speed or less, to make your intentions obvious to the other vessel. The next paragraph of the Rule suggests that a course alteration is often better than an alteration of speed.

> c.   If there is sufficient sea room, alteration of course alone may be the most effective action to avoid a close-quarters situation provided that it is made in good time, is substantial and does not result in another close-quarters situation.

This part of the Rule refers to **close-quarters** situations rather than just to **collision** situations. What constitutes a close-quarters situation depends not only on the size of the vessels concerned, but also on the visibility at the time. Two large tankers approaching each other in open water, even in good visibility, would probably consider two miles to be a close-quarters situation. But two yachts or fishing boats, which are obviously much more manoeuvrable, would probably not consider two miles to be close under the same conditions.

If two vessels are in sight of one another, it will then generally be considered safe to pass closer to each other than if they have detected each other only by radar. It is often much easier to assess a situation more accurately when you can actually see the other vessel, than if you are plotting it on the radar. In restricted visibility, approaching another vessel within two or three miles might be considered to be close-quarters, whereas in clear visibility, perhaps a mile would be quite acceptable.

When deciding whether to alter course, there are a number of factors to consider. This paragraph warns us to ensure that there is sufficient sea room. It would probably not be a good idea to alter course 90° if your vessel is proceeding up a narrow channel! It also warns us not to alter into another close-quarters situation, so have a good look around for other vessels before putting the wheel over.

When we get to **Rule 17**, we shall see that, except in restricted visibility, when two vessels are approaching, there is a period when the stand-on vessel should not make any alterations, but must hold her course and speed.

In **Rule 19**, we shall see that in restricted visibility, we are told that as far as possible we must avoid making a turn to port for a vessel forward of the beam, except when overtaking, and we should try to avoid altering course towards a vessel abeam, or abaft the beam. Generally speaking these are good rules to follow in clear visibility too. It is nearly always safer to alter to starboard for vessels ahead, so we pass port-to-port, and in the other situations, it is generally safer to make the turn away from the other vessel, rather than towards it.

> d.   Action taken to avoid collision with another vessel shall be such as to result in passing at a safe distance. The effectiveness of the action shall be carefully checked until the other vessel is finally past and clear.

When two vessels are approaching, and they can see each other, then the onus is on the give-way vessel to ensure that the passing distance is sufficient to be considered safe. When the visibility is restricted, and the two vessels are not in sight, then we will see under **Rule 19** there are no "stand-on" vessels. Any vessel which detects another vessel by radar alone is obliged to take avoiding action to prevent a close-quarters situation arising, so both vessels would be obliged to ensure that the passing distance was safe.

What constitutes a safe distance obviously depends on circumstances. For two large vessels meeting in the open sea, in good visibility, a mile might be considered a safe distance. In reduced visibility it might be considered that 3 miles would be a safe distance. In a narrow channel, vessels would have to pass each other at much closer distances. Smaller, very manoeuvrable vessels can generally pass at closer distances in safety than larger, less manoeuvrable vessels.

By passing at a "safe distance", rather than just barely missing the other vessel, the give-way vessel is more likely to make to make her intentions obvious to the other vessel, and reduce the chances of any misunderstanding.

The second part of this paragraph warns us that we must continue to monitor the situation until the other vessel is **past and clear**. If the other vessel is being tracked on radar, then it should continue to be plotted until it is well clear. If it is in sight visually, bearings should continue to be taken until it is well clear. This is to ensure that the other vessel is behaving as you anticipated, and does not suddenly do something unexpected, to put you back on a collision course.

For example, you may be plotting another vessel, in restricted visibility, approaching at a relatively high speed, fine on your port bow. The plot shows that it will pass less than a mile away, on your starboard bow. You do not consider this to be a safe distance, and **Rule 19** says you must take action. If you were to alter course to starboard, you would be crossing his bows – not a safe thing to do. If you altered to port, to increase the passing distance, there is a possibility that he will correctly alter course to starboard, to try to pass you port-to-port. This would put you on a collision course. Probably the safest thing to do is to reduce speed, to increase the passing distance. However, you must continue the plot, because if he were to alter to starboard, you would have to increase speed again, or risk being on a collision course.

If you are the give-way vessel, perhaps in an overtaking situation, your responsibility to keep clear of the other vessel exists until you are past and clear. You cannot overtake another vessel, perhaps on his starboard side, and then as soon as you are past his bows, alter hard to port, to put the vessels into a crossing situation, where the other vessel suddenly becomes the give-way vessel. Your responsibility to keep clear exists until you are **past and clear**.

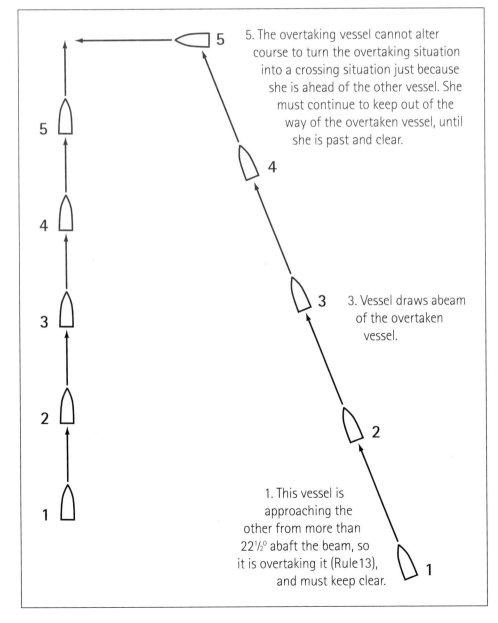

5. The overtaking vessel cannot alter course to turn the overtaking situation into a crossing situation just because she is ahead of the other vessel. She must continue to keep out of the way of the overtaken vessel, until she is past and clear.

3. Vessel draws abeam of the overtaken vessel.

1. This vessel is approaching the other from more than 22½° abaft the beam, so it is overtaking it (Rule 13), and must keep clear.

Figure 8.3. The give-way vessel, in this case the overtaking vessel, has the responsibility to keep out of the way of the other vessel until it is safely past and clear of that vessel. It cannot turn an overtaking situation into a crossing situation.

> e.   If necessary to avoid collision or to allow more time to assess the situation, a vessel shall slacken her speed or take all way off by stopping or reversing her means of propulsion.

We have already seen that **Rule 6** says we must always proceed at a safe speed, and what constitutes a safe speed will vary with circumstances and conditions. The watchkeeper must understand the operation of the engines, and be able to reduce speed, or indeed increase speed if required. This paragraph says that we should slacken speed if necessary to avoid a collision. Under some circumstances, an increase in speed may be helpful, to avoid a close-quarters situation, or indeed, a collision, but generally speaking, if there is doubt about how a situation is developing, it is usually best to slow down, or stop. This is not only likely to give more time to assess the situation, but it will also minimise damage if a collision becomes inevitable!

Rule 5 told us that we must make a full appraisal of the situation and of the risk of collision, and **Rule 7** that we must not make assumptions on the basis of scanty information. If another vessel is sighted at short range, often the only way to get sufficient time to make a proper assessment is to slow down or stop. This is not only a matter of good seamanship, but this part of the rule says we **shall** slow down if necessary, to allow time to assess the situation. This requirement is not limited to power driven vessels – it also applies to sailing vessels. They too **shall** slow down if necessary to avoid a collision, or to give extra time to assess the situation.

The Rule uses the term **reversing her means of propulsion** to take into account those vessels which go astern by means of variable pitch propellers, as well as those which go astern by changing the direction of the propeller. Whatever method is used to "reverse the means of propulsion", we will see in **Rule 34** that if we are in sight of another vessel, and we **operate astern propulsion** to manoeuvre according to the Rules, then we **shall** sound the appropriate signal on the whistle, which is three short blasts. It is important to note that it is obligatory to sound the signal; it is not at our discretion.

A single screw vessel will usually slew to one side when making a stop using astern propulsion. Which direction she slews depends upon the direction of rotation of the propeller when going astern. The watchkeeper must be aware of which direction the vessel is likely to turn when astern propulsion is engaged.

> f. i.   A vessel which, by any of these Rules, is required not to impede the passage or safe passage of another vessel shall, when required by the circumstances of the case, take early action to allow sufficient sea room for the safe passage of the other vessel.

There are several Rules which require vessels **not to impede the passage, or not to impede the safe passage** of another vessel. **Rule 9**, (<u>N</u>ine – <u>N</u>arrow channels), **Rule 10**, (<u>T</u>en – <u>T</u>raffic separation schemes) and **Rule 18** (Responsibilities between vessels, or what can be thought of as the "pecking order" of vessels) all require vessels not to impede the passage, or the safe passage of another vessel.

Paragraph a. of this Rule told us that any action we might take to avoid a collision should be **positive**, and **made in ample time**. Now this sub-paragraph is telling us that whenever we are required to **not impede the passage**, or to **not impede the safe passage** of another vessel, then we must **take early action to allow sufficient sea room** for the other vessel. It is telling us that we must act before there is a risk of collision, to allow sufficient room for the vessel whose passage is not to be impeded.

> ii.   A vessel required not to impede the passage or safe passage of another vessel is not relieved of this obligation if approaching the other vessel so as to involve risk of collision and shall, when taking action, have full regard to the action which may be required by the Rules of this part.

A vessel which is required not to impede the passage of another vessel does not lose this obligation, even if a risk of collision develops, and the other vessel becomes the give-way vessel. It must continue to try and manoeuvre in a manner which allows sufficient sea room for the safe passage of the other vessel. The vessel which was required to not impede the passage of the other vessel must manoeuvre in accordance with the normal steering Rules, and must consider how the other vessel is likely to manoeuvre, also in accordance with the normal steering Rules, which, as we shall see in the next paragraph, she is bound to do.

> iii.   A vessel, the passage of which is not to be impeded, remains fully obliged to comply with the Rules of this part when the two vessels are approaching one another so as to involve risk of collision.

This sub-paragraph views the same situation from the perspective of the other vessel, i.e. the one whose passage was not to be impeded. If a vessel is in a situation where it has the right to not have its passage impeded, and another vessel approaches so as to cause a risk of collision, then despite having a right to not have its passage impeded, the vessel must manoeuvre in accordance with the normal steering Rules, to avoid a collision.

So just because a vessel is navigating in a narrow channel, or a traffic separation scheme, or is perhaps constrained by its draught, it cannot ignore the movements of other vessels. It must still assess any developing risk of collision, and be prepared to manoeuvre to avoid a collision, in accordance with the normal steering Rules.

Summary of Rule 8 – Action to Avoid a Collision.

1. *When manoeuvring to avoid a collision, the actions must be* **positive, made in ample time,** *and in accordance with* **good seamanship.**
2. *Any alteration of course and/or speed must be large enough to be apparent to the other vessel either visually or by radar (30° to 60° for a course alteration, and slow to half speed or less, if reducing speed). Slowing down can give more time to assess the situation, and remember to give three short blasts if engaging astern propulsion, if in sight of the other vessel.*
3. *A* **substantial** *alteration of course,* **made in good time,** *is often the best way for the give-way vessel to avoid a close-quarters situation, provided there is sea room and no conflicting vessels. The actions must result in passing at a* **safe distance,** *and the situation must be monitored until the other vessel is* **past and clear.**
4. *A vessel required to* **not impede the passage** *of another vessel must take early action to allow sufficient sea room for the safe passage of the other vessel. This obligation continues even if a risk of collision develops, and the other vessel becomes the give-way vessel. <u>Both vessels are required to manoeuvre according to the normal steering rules if a risk of collision develops.</u>*

Rule 9. Narrow Channels
(Rule **N**ine concerns **N**arrow channels)

This Rule applies to vessels navigating in narrow channels, which are connected with the high seas, and navigable by seagoing vessels, unless there is a conflicting local Rule, imposed by the Coastal State, in whose waters the channel lies. It does not apply to traffic separation schemes, even though some of them may be narrow. We shall see that **Rule 10** deals specifically with traffic separation schemes.

> a.   A vessel proceeding along the course of a narrow channel or fairway shall keep as near to the outer limit of the channel or fairway which lies on her starboard side as is safe and practicable.

Vessels must navigate on the starboard side when proceeding along the course of a narrow channel or fairway. This is consistent with passing approaching vessels port-to-port. Vessels are not expected to put themselves at risk by passing dangerously close to shoals or obstructions, and how close to the edge of the channel a vessel navigates, is obviously dependent on the draught of the vessel. Shallower draught vessels will generally be expected

to navigate closer to the edge than deeper draught vessels, but all vessels are expected to navigate on the starboard side of the channel. It is not enough to move to the starboard side on sighting another vessel. The Rule does not of course prohibit vessels crossing the channel or fairway, but paragraph d. places some obligations on crossing vessels.

The slightly complicated bit of this Rule is to determine what constitutes a narrow channel or fairway. There is no hard and fast definition of a narrow channel. There is no minimum length nor minimum width for a narrow channel, and it may even extend beyond the last navigational aids which are marking the channel. A channel which is such that the navigation of a vessel in the channel is restricted, will usually be regarded as a narrow channel. A recommended route between a series of buoys, where a vessel could safely navigate outside the limits of the marked route, would not be regarded as a narrow channel, but good seamanship would still suggest navigating on the starboard side of the recommended route.

A fairway could be a dredged channel maintained by the port authority, or it could be a deep water channel marked on the chart, for the use of deep draught vessels.

If there is doubt about the status of a particular channel, treat it as a narrow channel or fairway, and it is almost always safest to navigate on the starboard side of any channel.

> b.   A vessel of less than 20 metres in length or a sailing vessel shall not impede the passage of a vessel which can safely navigate only within a narrow channel or fairway.

Sailing vessels, and any vessels less than 20 metres are not allowed to **impede the passage** of a vessel which can only navigate within the narrow channel or fairway. It makes sense that smaller, more manoeuvrable vessels should not get in the way of larger vessels, which can safely navigate only within the channel. A small shallow draught vessel can often be safely navigated outside of a channel, and generally this would be the best thing for a small vessel to do. To avoid confusing on-coming vessels, it is safest to navigate along the starboard side of the channel, so any vessels approaching in the opposite direction are passed port-to-port.

A sailing vessel, because of the direction of the wind, may not be able to navigate only on the starboard side of the channel. However, it is not allowed to **impede the passage** of any vessel which can only navigate within the confines of the narrow channel or fairway.

In **Rule 8. f.** we saw that a vessel which must not impede the passage of another vessel must **take early action to allow sufficient sea room for the safe passage of the other vessel,** so this applies to any sailing vessel, regardless of size, and any other type of vessel less than 20 metres in length, which is navigating in a narrow channel or fairway.

Vessels under 20 metres and sailing vessels are required to not impede the passage of vessels **which can safely navigate only within the narrow channel or fairway**. It is not only the passage of vessels which are showing the signals that they are constrained by their draught which must not be impeded, but **any vessel which can safely navigate only within the narrow channel or fairway** must be allowed a clear passage.

> c.   A vessel engaged in fishing shall not impede the passage of any other vessel navigating within a narrow channel or fairway.

Unless prohibited by a local law, vessels are allowed to fish within the confines of a narrow channel or fairway, but they must **take early action to allow sufficient sea room for the safe passage of other vessels** which are navigating in the narrow channel or fairway. Fishing vessels are not allowed to impede the passage of **any** vessel navigating in the channel or fairway, so this includes small vessels under 20 metres and sailing vessels which are navigating in the narrow channel or fairway.

> d.   A vessel shall not cross a narrow channel or fairway if such crossing impedes the passage of a vessel which can safely navigate only within such channel or fairway. The latter vessel may use the sound signal prescribed in Rule 34 (d) if in doubt as to the intention of the crossing vessel.

A vessel **shall not cross** a narrow channel or fairway if the crossing will impede the passage of a vessel which can safely navigate only within the narrow channel or fairway. So a vessel wanting to cross the channel must wait for an opportune moment to make the crossing, so as not to impede the passage of vessels which can only navigate within the channel.

If the vessel in the channel or fairway can safely navigate outside the channel or fairway, then normal crossing Rules apply: the vessel which has the other on her starboard bow gives way.

A vessel which can only navigate in the narrow channel or fairway, which has any doubt as to the intentions of a crossing vessel, should sound at least five short blasts on the whistle to express this doubt – this is often referred to as the "wake-up signal", and this is the signal that the Rule refers us to in **Rule 34.d.**

> e.   i. In a narrow channel or fairway when overtaking can take place only if the vessel to be overtaken has to take action to permit safe passing, the vessel intending to overtake shall indicate her

> intention by sounding the appropriate signal prescribed in Rule 34 (c) (i). The vessel to be overtaken shall, if in agreement, sound the appropriate signal prescribed in Rule 34 (c) (ii) and take steps to permit safe passing. If in doubt she may sound the signal prescribed in Rule 34 (d).

Rule 9 generally applies in all conditions of visibility, but the sound signals referred to in **Rule 34** are to be used only when vessels are in sight of each other, so the implication is that this part of **Rule 9** applies only when vessels are in sight of each other, and not when the vessels can "see" each other only by radar.

The whistle signals for overtaking are:
- Two prolonged and a short blast – I intend to overtake you on your starboard side.
- Two prolonged and two short blasts – I intend to overtake you on your port side.

(These signals are easy to learn if you remember that the overtaking signals start with two prolonged blasts, then as with the manoeuvring signals, one short blast means you are altering to starboard and two short blasts means altering to port.)

The vessel which is about to be overtaken, if she agrees, sounds:
- One prolonged, one short, one prolonged and one short blast.

This is Morse code for the letter "C" (–·–·), which is the International Code for "Affirmative". (I remember this by thinking that "C" sounds like the Spanish "Si", which means yes.)

If she does not agree to be overtaken, or is in doubt, then the vessel about to be overtaken sounds:
- At least five short and rapid blasts

This is the usual signal for "I do not understand your intentions", and is often called the "Wake-up signal".

When we look at **Rule 34** in detail, we will see that the whistle signals can be supplemented by light signals.

It would be a matter of good seamanship for the vessel being overtaken to not only move to the side of the channel, but also to slow down, in order to reduce the time that the two vessels might be running close together.

It is very common practice to use the VHF radio to discuss and agree an overtaking manoeuvre in narrow channels. Generally there is no problem with identifying the other vessel, either by being close enough to read her name, or by indicating her proximity to a particular navigation mark. Particularly in the USA, you will often hear the Captain of one vessel informing another that he will pass "on two whistles" – this means that he intends to pass on the port side.

Some Coastal States have gone so far as to implement their own local rule, which specifically authorises the use of the VHF radio in these circumstances, for vessels in their waters.

In more open situations, it is often difficult to identify the other vessel, and trying to call them by VHF can either waste time which could be better spent initiating a manoeuvre, or can lead to ambiguity, if the wrong vessel answers the call. Unless the other vessel can be easily identified, it is better to rely on the whistle signals.

> ii.   This Rule does not relieve the overtaking vessel of her obligation under Rule 13.

Rule 13 basically says that an overtaking vessel shall keep out of the way of the vessel being overtaken. Just because an overtaking vessel has sounded the appropriate signal that she is about to overtake, it does not give her any special right of way. She must still keep out of the way of the overtaken vessel, and if this is likely to prove difficult, then perhaps she should not overtake.

In neither section of this paragraph is there any mention of the term "power-driven vessel", so this Rule is equally applicable to sailing vessels and to power-driven vessels, and indeed all other types of vessels. Sailing vessels are expected to sound the same signals, and when we look at **Rule 13** – the overtaking Rule, in detail, we will see that if a sailing vessel is overtaking a power-driven vessel, the sailing vessel must keep clear.

> f.   A vessel nearing a bend or an area of a narrow channel or fairway where other vessels may be obscured by an intervening obstruction shall navigate with particular alertness and caution and shall sound the appropriate signal prescribed in Rule 34 (e).

The signal in **Rule 34 (e)** is one prolonged blast. The Rule says we **shall** sound the appropriate signal when approaching a bend or obstruction, not just if we feel like it. Whenever we are approaching a bend or an obstruction where other vessels, particularly small vessels could be obscured, then we <u>must</u> sound the signal.

It also says that we **shall** navigate with **particular alertness and caution** when approaching a bend. It does not say that we should do this only if another vessel is coming, it says that we must do it always, when approaching a bend.

The very first paragraph of **Rule 9** told us that we have to navigate on the starboard side of the channel, so when approaching a left hand bend in the channel, it would be wrong for us to cut the corner, and move over to the port side of the channel, just because we did not think that there was another vessel approaching. This paragraph is reinforcing this, by saying that we **shall** navigate with **particular alertness and caution** when approaching a

bend. This would be taken to include staying on the starboard side of the channel.

If a vessel approaching a bend in a narrow channel hears a prolonged blast from another vessel, they must answer it with a prolonged blast of their own.

If there is a significant current flowing in the channel, it would generally be a matter of good seamanship for the vessel going into the current to slow down and wait for the other vessel to pass. The vessel going into the current will generally have much more control over her steering than the vessel travelling down-stream, with the current. Many Coastal States which have large rivers in their jurisdiction have instigated local rules, which specifically give the right of way to vessels travelling with the current.

> g.   Any vessel shall, if the circumstances of the case admit, avoid anchoring in a narrow channel.

It is pretty obvious that a vessel anchoring in a narrow channel is likely to impede the safe passage of other vessels, so it should only be done in the case of emergency, or if it is absolutely required by the nature of the work of the vessel, for example repairing or replacing a navigation mark or underwater cable. In such a situation, warnings should be transmitted on the appropriate VHF channel, probably on channels 16 and/or 13.

Reduced visibility would not normally be an acceptable reason for a vessel to anchor in a narrow channel. There is a likelihood that other vessels will continue to navigate using radar, and a small vessel which is not equipped with radar should not enter the channel if there is a chance of being forced to stop by reduced visibility. If the visibility is unexpectedly reduced, and the vessel is forced to anchor, then it must do so out of the channel, if this is possible.

Summary of Rule 9 – Narrow Channels.

(Nine for Narrow Channels)

1. *All vessels must navigate on the starboard side of a narrow channel or fairway.*
2. *Vessels of less than 20 metres in length, or sailing vessels must not impede the passage of <u>vessels which can only navigate safely in the channel</u>, and fishing boats must not impede the passage of <u>any vessels</u> navigating in the channel.*
3. *No vessel may cross a narrow channel or fairway if the crossing impedes the passage of a vessel which can only navigate safely in the channel. For vessels which can navigate outside the channel, then normal crossing Rules apply.*
4. *A vessel in sight of another, wishing to overtake in a narrow channel or fairway, and needing the co-operation of the other vessel, shall sound the appropriate signals (Two long and a short to overtake to starboard, two long and two shorts to overtake to port.) The vessel to be overtaken signals her agreement by sounding "C"*

(Long, short, long and short) or her disagreement or doubt, by sounding at least five short and rapid blasts. Normal overtaking Rules still apply – the overtaking vessel must keep clear.

5. *Approaching a blind bend, vessels must stay on the starboard side of the channel, and sound a prolonged blast. This should be answered with a prolonged blast by any other approaching vessel which hears the signal.*

6. *Do not anchor in a narrow channel if it can possibly be avoided.*

7. *Local rules often give the right of way to vessels travelling with the current in swift flowing rivers.*

Rule 10. Traffic separation schemes

(Rule **T**en concerns **T**raffic separation schemes)

> a. This Rule applies to traffic separation schemes adopted by the Organisation and does not relieve any vessel of her obligation under any other Rule.

There are many kinds of traffic separation schemes. Some traffic separation schemes may require that all vessels use the scheme, while others may specify that only particular types of vessels must use the scheme. The use of other schemes may be voluntary.

The Organisation referred to is the International Maritime Organisation, the IMO. So theoretically, **Rule 10** applies only to those traffic separation schemes which have been approved by the IMO. However, **Rule 2 a.** told us that we have to act with good seamanship, and it could hardly be construed to be good seamanship if one were to ignore a traffic separation scheme because it had not been adopted by the IMO. It would generally be good practice to follow any recommended traffic separation scheme.

This first paragraph makes it absolutely plain that just because a vessel is navigating in a traffic separation scheme, it does not acquire any extra right of way over other vessels. Generally, if a vessel navigating within a traffic lane sees a crossing vessel on her starboard side, then **Rule 15** still applies, and the vessel within the lane must give way to the crossing vessel. However, we will see in part **j.** of this Rule that vessels under 20 metres, and sailing vessels must not impede the passage of a power-driven vessel following a traffic lane.

Figure 10.1 Nomenclature used in a Traffic Separation Scheme

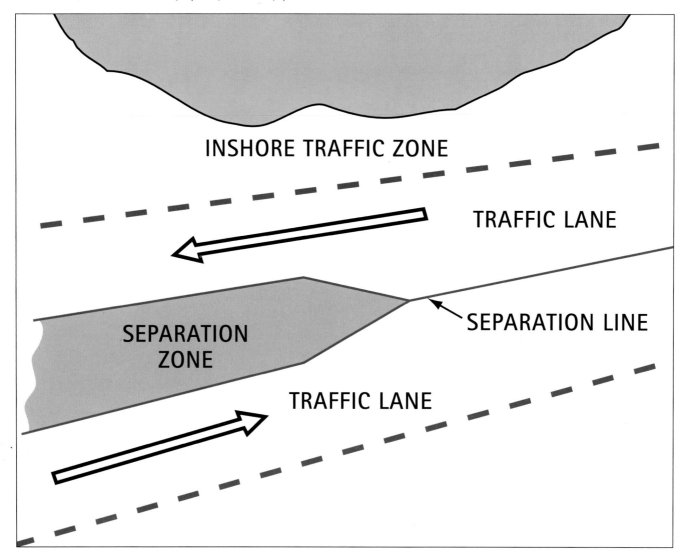

b.   A vessel using a traffic separation scheme shall:

i. proceed in the appropriate traffic lane in the general direction of traffic flow for that lane;

ii. so far as practicable keep clear of a traffic separation line or separation zone;

iii. normally join or leave a traffic lane at the termination of a lane, but when joining or leaving from either side shall do so at as small an angle to the general direction of traffic flow as practicable.

A vessel is assumed to be using a traffic separation scheme if she is navigating within the limits of the scheme, but is not crossing the lanes, nor fishing within the central separation zones.

All vessels, and this applies to sailing vessels as well as power-driven vessels, which are navigating within a traffic lane must follow the general direction of the traffic flow. There are arrows on the chart, within the lanes, depicting the direction of traffic flow. It is not necessary to follow a direction exactly parallel to these arrows, but neither is it permitted to go in an opposite direction to the arrows. The arrows are not meant to suggest a particular route within the lane, only the general direction of the flow of traffic.

Between adjacent traffic lanes, there is a separation line, or, more often, a separation zone. Vessels using the scheme must, so far as is practicable, keep clear of this line or zone. Very often the edges of the traffic lanes are not marked with buoys, so it is not easy to tell when a vessel is straying into the other lane where it could suddenly face oncoming traffic. By navigating away from the edge of the lane, there is a margin allowing for error. Obviously vessels crossing the scheme can enter the separation zone, and we will see that with some restrictions, fishing boats are allowed to operate within the separation zone, but all other vessels should keep clear of the separation zone.

When a vessel is navigating in a traffic separation scheme, it is important that the position of the vessel be continuously monitored, so as to ensure that it navigates within the confines of the lane at all times, and does not stray into the separation zone, or even worse, into the opposing lane.

Vessels entering the traffic separation scheme are supposed to enter at the ends of the lanes wherever possible. If that is not practicable, then vessels are allowed to enter part-way along a lane, but they must do so at a shallow angle, in the direction of flow of the traffic. Entering at a shallow angle helps other traffic recognise that the other vessel is not trying to cross the lane, which as we shall see, must be done at right angles to the flow of the traffic.

Figure 10.2   a. Acceptable routes for vessels entering or leaving a traffic lane.
                b. Examples of incorrect routes for entering or leaving a traffic lane.

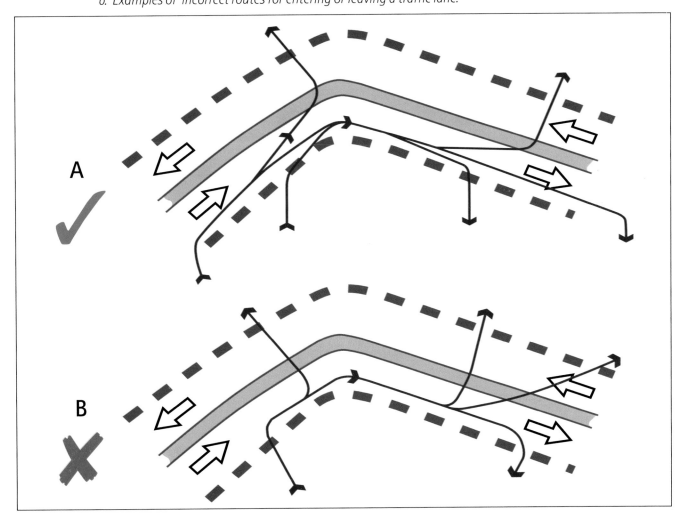

> c.   A vessel shall, so far as practicable, avoid crossing traffic lanes but if obliged to do so shall cross on a heading as nearly as practicable at right angles to the general direction of traffic flow.

Vessels must try to avoid crossing traffic lanes whenever possible. There is unlikely to be any justification for crossing very short lanes, such as might be found off a headland. Vessels would be expected to go around the extremities of such short lanes.

If a traffic separation zone extends over several miles, then it can be expected that there will be vessels crossing the traffic lanes. This part of the Rule states that crossing vessels must do so **on a heading as nearly as practicable at right angles to the general direction of the traffic flow**. It should be noted that it does not say "if traffic is using the lane" or any words to that effect. Crossing vessels are expected to cross at right angles regardless of whether there is traffic in the lane or not.

Note that the requirement is for the <u>heading</u> to be at right angles, not the track, so vessels crossing are expected to <u>steer</u> at right angles to the direction of traffic flow. If the crossing vessel is slow, and there is a current, the track

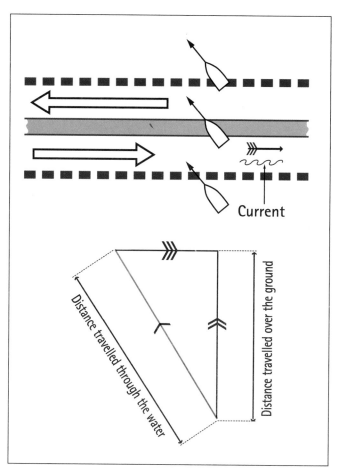

Fig 10.3

b. *Incorrect. Vessel allowing for the current, to make a track at right angles across a Traffic Separation Scheme. This results in taking a longer time to clear the scheme, as it has to go farther through the water.*

made good could be far from right angles to the lane. By steering at right angles, the vessel will clear the lane in the shortest possible time. If the track were at right angles, allowing for the effect of the current, the crossing vessel would have to travel farther through the water, and so take longer to cross the lane.

It is worth noting again that, just because a vessel is navigating in a traffic lane, it does not acquire any special right of way. **Rule 15** – Crossing situations, applies at all times when two vessels are in sight of one-another: a vessel which has another vessel on her starboard side must keep out of the way of that vessel. We will see in paragraphs **i.** and **j.** that there are a few exceptions. Fishing vessels, vessels less than 20 metres in length and sailing vessels, must not impede the passage of vessels navigating in a traffic lane. If such vessels want to cross a lane, or indeed are themselves navigating within a lane, they must keep out of the way of any other vessels that are following a lane.

It may be that a vessel wishes to cross only one of a pair of lanes. This is permitted provided that the vessel enters or leaves the lane in which it is travelling, at a shallow angle, and crosses the other lane at right angles.

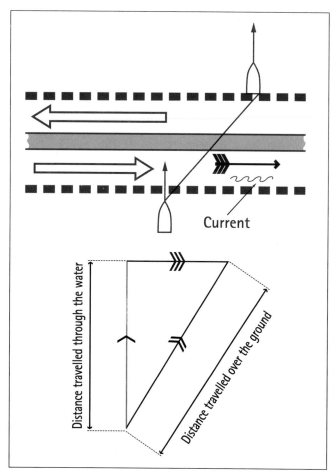

Fig 10.3

a. *Vessel heading at right angles across a Traffic Separation Scheme, with track over the ground at an angle because of a current.*

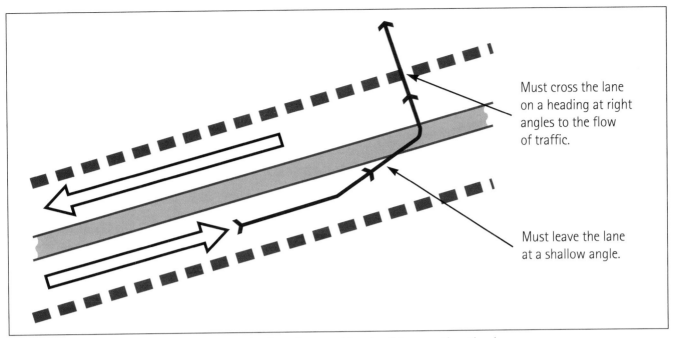

Fig 10.4 Vessel travelling for part of the length of one lane, and leaving it to cross the other lane.

Must cross the lane on a heading at right angles to the flow of traffic.

Must leave the lane at a shallow angle.

> d. i. A vessel shall not use an inshore traffic zone when it can safely use the appropriate traffic lane within the adjacent traffic separation scheme. However, vessels of less than 20 metres in length, sailing vessels and vessels engaged in fishing may use the inshore traffic zone.

In some traffic separation schemes, there are inshore traffic zones established beside the traffic lanes. If they have been established, they are marked on the chart.

If a traffic separation scheme is situated off a headland, there may be an inshore traffic zone situated between the nearest traffic lane and the land. There would then be the possibility of vessels having three choices. They could pass through the inshore traffic zone, follow the appropriate traffic lane, or stay well clear by passing outside the separation scheme altogether.

However, when a traffic separation scheme is established in a strait or channel, there is a possibility that there will be two inshore traffic zones, one between each traffic lane and its corresponding coast, so vessels must either pass along the traffic lanes or through one of the inshore traffic zones.

The inshore traffic zone may well be narrow, and to reduce congestion and the chance of collision, this part of the Rule says that vessels must use the appropriate traffic lane whenever possible, and as far as possible, to avoid using the inshore traffic zones. Power-driven vessels under 20 metres, sailing vessels and vessels engaged in fishing are exempted. These vessels are allowed to use the inshore traffic zones at any time. However, any vessel which might enter or leave a traffic lane, when entering or leaving an inshore traffic zone, must do so in accordance with paragraph **b. iii.**, which says they must do so at as small an angle to the general direction of traffic flow as practicable.

The Rule then goes on to give more exemptions where vessels may use the inshore traffic zone:

> ii. Notwithstanding subparagraph (d) (i), a vessel may use an inshore traffic zone when *en route* to or from a port, offshore installation or structure, pilot station or any other place situated within the inshore traffic zone, or to avoid immediate danger.

Vessels *en route* to, or from, a port, offshore installation or structure, pilot station or any other place situated within the inshore traffic zone, may use the inshore traffic zone. So effectively the inshore traffic zones are prohibited to through traffic only if they are power-driven vessels of more than 20 metres. Coastal traffic, that is, vessels going to or from a port or pilot station etc. located within the zone, can use the inshore traffic zone.

Any vessel is permitted to enter an inshore traffic zone to avoid immediate danger. There would have to be some special circumstance, such as breakdown or some similar emergency, for this to be acceptable. Taking a short-cut by cutting a corner would not be a valid reason!

> e. A vessel other than a crossing vessel or a vessel joining or leaving a lane shall not normally enter a separation zone or cross a separation line except:
> i. in cases of emergency to avoid immediate danger,
> ii. to engage in fishing within a separation zone.

A separation zone is the area between adjacent traffic lanes, which is there to increase the separation between traffic that is going in opposite directions. Separation zones are also sometimes used between traffic lanes and inshore traffic zones, to provide a buffer zone between them.

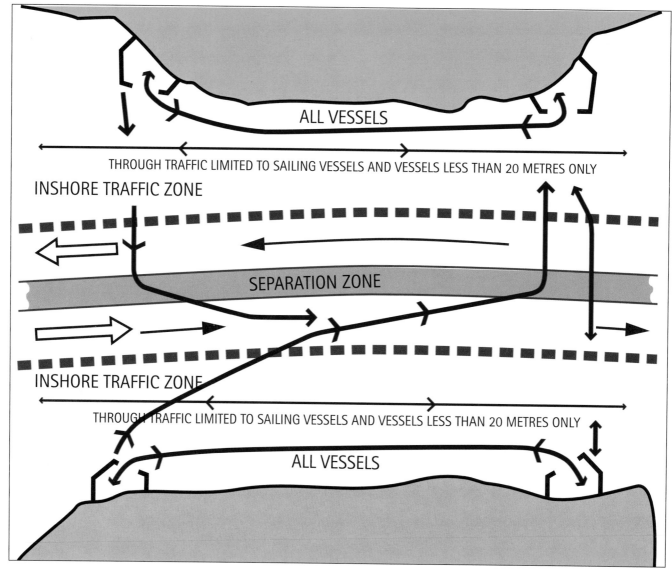

Fig 10.5 Illustration of Traffic Separation Scheme and Inshore Traffic Zones, showing a selection of permitted routes for various vessels.

Separation zones are marked on the chart which shows the traffic separation scheme.

Under normal circumstances, only vessels crossing a traffic separation scheme, or vessels joining or leaving a traffic lane are permitted to enter a separation zone. Vessels fishing, and vessels which because of some special circumstance need to enter the separation zone to avoid immediate danger are exempted from this restriction.

When vessels are fishing in a separation zone, they must be careful that neither they nor their gear impedes the passage of a vessel navigating in the adjacent lane – we will see that this is stipulated in **paragraph i.** of this Rule. Since there is not supposed to be any through-traffic navigating within the separation zone, there is no general direction of traffic movement within the zone, so the fishing vessels are free to move in any direction within the zone. However, if fishing vessels pass through traffic lanes to enter or leave the separation zone, they must enter and leave the traffic lanes in compliance with **paragraph b. iii.** which says that vessels entering or leaving a traffic lane

must do so at as small an angle to the general direction of traffic flow as is practicable.

> f.   A vessel navigating in areas near the terminations of traffic separation schemes shall do so with particular caution.

Traffic separation lanes reduce the risk of collisions between vessels navigating within the lanes, but at the ends of the lanes, because of a concentration of converging and diverging traffic, there is probably an increased risk of collision. Extra vigilance is called for when navigating near the ends of the traffic separation scheme, both from vessels navigating within the scheme, as well as from those which are passing close to the scheme. This is especially true if the visibility is restricted.

> g.   A vessel shall so far as practicable avoid anchoring in a traffic separation scheme or in areas near its terminations.

A vessel anchoring within a traffic lane might impede the passage of vessels navigating within the lane, and it could also cause confusion among approaching traffic, if the wind or a current caused the vessel to lie in a direction other than that of the general flow of traffic.

Note that the prohibition covers the whole of the separation scheme, not just the traffic lanes themselves, so vessels are also precluded from anchoring in the separation zones. In **paragraph e.** we saw that under exceptional circumstances, **to avoid immediate danger**, vessels are allowed to navigate in the separation zones. Under similar exceptional circumstances, they would be allowed to anchor there as well, for example if the vessel suffered an engine breakdown.

This paragraph, and basic good seamanship, both suggest that vessels should not anchor near the ends of the traffic lanes. These areas will generally have a high density of traffic converging on the ends of the lanes, and vessels anchored there can only lead to confusion, and increase any possible risk of collision.

We will see in **paragraphs k. and l.** of this Rule that vessels which are required to work within the area of the traffic separation scheme are exempt from complying with the Rule. Such vessels are allowed to anchor within the traffic separation scheme, while completing their work.

> h.   A vessel not using a traffic separation scheme shall avoid it by as wide a margin as is practicable.

Paragraph c. states that vessels may cross traffic separation schemes if it is impracticable to go around them, provided that they cross the traffic lanes at right angles to the general direction of flow of traffic. Other vessels which are not using the scheme, must pass well clear of it. There would be an increased risk of collision if vessels passed close to the boundary of a traffic lane, but in the opposite direction to traffic which is navigating within the lane.

> i.   A vessel engaged in fishing shall not impede the passage of any vessel following a traffic lane.

We have already seen that vessels are allowed to fish in separation zones, and in inshore traffic zones, and this paragraph implies that they are allowed to fish in the traffic lanes as well. However, vessels which are fishing within a traffic separation scheme must **not impede the passage of any vessel following a traffic lane**, so they must manoeuvre in such a way that vessels may pass easily, without them having to leave the traffic lane.

Although vessels are allowed to fish in the traffic lanes, they are not exempt from complying with the Rules of the traffic separation scheme, so when fishing within a traffic lane, they must proceed in the general direction of the flow of the traffic. They are not allowed to go in the opposite direction to the traffic when in a traffic lane.

> j.   A vessel of less than 20 metres in length or a sailing vessel shall not impede the safe passage of a power-driven vessel following a traffic lane.

Whether crossing a traffic lane, or navigating along a lane, power-driven vessels of less than 20 metres and sailing vessels of any size are not allowed to impede the safe passage of a power-driven vessel following a traffic lane.

Power-driven vessels of less than 20 metres and sailing vessels are allowed to use the inshore traffic zone at all times – **paragraph d. i.**, and it is often safest for them to do so. They do not then risk impeding the safe passage of larger vessels navigating in a traffic lane.

If the wind is such that a sailing vessel cannot easily navigate in the general direction of the traffic flow within a traffic lane, then it should either navigate in the inshore traffic zone, as is permitted under **paragraph d. i.**, or it should stay well clear of the scheme. Alternatively, if it has an auxiliary engine, it should use this, and become a power-driven vessel while within the boundaries of the scheme.

Any vessel which is required not to impede the passage of another vessel must navigate in accordance with **Rule 8. f.**, which states that the vessel must **take early action to allow sufficient sea room for the safe passage of the other vessel.**

> k.   A vessel restricted in her ability to manoeuvre when engaged in an operation for the maintenance of safety of navigation in a traffic separation scheme is exempted from complying with this Rule to the extent necessary to carry out the operation.

Vessels whose work involves the maintenance of buoys or navigation aids are exempted from complying with the Rule, as necessary to complete their work. Such vessels would normally be classed as restricted in their ability to manoeuvre, and would be expected to display the appropriate signals. The next paragraph allows other vessels to work within the boundaries of the traffic separation scheme.

> l.   A vessel restricted in her ability to manoeuvre when engaged in an operation for the laying, servicing or picking up of a submarine cable, within a traffic separation scheme, is exempted from complying with this Rule to the extent necessary to carry out the operation.

As with vessels required to work on navigation aids or buoys within the scheme, vessels are allowed to work on submarine cables which pass through the scheme.

In both cases, the vessels concerned would be expected to show the signals for "Restricted in their ability to manoeuvre" – ball-diamond-ball by day, and red-white,-red at night, as stipulated in Rule 27. Also they would be expected to seek permission from the authority controlling the separation scheme before beginning their work. They should also warn other vessels of their operations by a Marine Advisory Notice, and by the transmission of *securité* announcements by radio.

These vessels would be allowed to anchor in a traffic lane or separation zone, and would even be allowed to navigate in a direction against the flow of traffic if it were absolutely necessary. However, they are expected to comply with the rules as far as they are able, and would not be allowed to navigate against the flow of traffic just to take a short cut. They would be expected to enter and leave traffic lanes in accordance with the rules, i.e. at their ends, or at a shallow angle in the direction of the general flow of traffic.

Summary of Rule10 – Traffic Separation Schemes.

(Ten for Traffic Separation Schemes)

1. *Vessels navigating in a traffic separation scheme assume no extra rights of way – the normal steering and sailing rules apply, except that power-driven vessels under 20 metres, sailing vessels and fishing vessels are not allowed to impede the safe passage of vessels navigating in a traffic lane.*
2. *Vessels must go in the direction of flow of a lane, and must join or leave the lane at the end, or at a shallow angle in the direction of the traffic flow. Vessels should not navigate close to the edge of a separation zone, nor should they enter a separation zone unless there is an emergency, the vessel is engaged in fishing, or it is crossing the scheme.*
3. *As far as possible, every vessel should avoid crossing a traffic separation scheme, but if it has to cross a lane, then it must do so on a heading which is at right angles to the general flow of traffic.*
4. *Through traffic is not allowed to use a designated inshore traffic zone, unless it is a sailing vessel or less than 20 metres. Through traffic must use the appropriate lane, or keep well clear of the scheme.*
5. *Fishing vessels are allowed to operate within a traffic separation scheme, but they must not impede the passage of vessels navigating in a traffic lane, nor must they navigate against the flow of traffic in a lane.*
6. *Vessels are allowed to work on navigation marks and submarine cables in a traffic separation scheme, at anchor if necessary, but they must seek permission, display the appropriate signals, and make their presence known by radio announcements. They are exempt from complying with any part of the Rule, as is necessary for their work, but must comply with other parts of the Rule, as far as possible. No other vessel is allowed to anchor within traffic lanes, near their ends, nor in separation zones except in the case of emergency.*
7. *All vessels must navigate with extreme caution near the ends of a traffic separation scheme.*

Part B.
STEERING AND SAILING RULES
Section TWO – Conduct of Vessels in Sight of One Another. (Rules 11–18)

Rule 11. Application

> Rules in this section apply to vessels in sight of one another.

Part B – the Steering and Sailing Rules, is divided into three sections. We have looked at **Section I**, which consisted of **Rules 4 to 10**. Those Rules apply <u>at all times</u>, in all conditions of visibility.

Now we are going to look at **Section II**, which covers **Rules 11 to 18**. As this Rule states, **Section II** applies only to vessels <u>in sight</u> of one another. They do not apply when a vessel has detected another vessel by radar, even if it found that a risk of collision exists, unless or until the vessel can also be seen visually.

Section III, which concerns vessels in <u>restricted visibility</u>, contains only **Rule 19**. We shall see that **Rule 19** applies whenever a vessel is detected by radar, but cannot be seen visually. If the vessels approach to the point where one can see the other, then **Rule 19** ceases to apply, and the Rules of **Section II**, namely **Rules 11 to 18**, come into force.

It is quite possible that when two vessels are approaching each other, they may not sight each other at the same instant. For example, one may have brighter navigation lights than the other, allowing it to be seen first. So it is entirely possible that one vessel may be navigating under **Section III**, i.e. **Rule 19**, while the other is applying the Rules of **Section II**. A vessel must comply with whichever section of the Rules apply at any given moment.

When we get to **Rule 19** – Vessels in Restricted Visibility, we will see that vessels not in sight of each other are discouraged from turning to port to avoid a vessel which has been detected by radar forward of the beam. This is to avoid any sudden conflict when the vessels do sight each other, perhaps at short range, and the Rules of **Section II** come into force. As we shall see shortly, give-way vessels will generally turn to starboard for vessels forward of the beam, so they pass port-to-port.

Vessels cannot claim that the Rules of **Section II** do not apply, just because a poor lookout is being kept. We have already seen in **Rule 5** that **every vessel shall at all times maintain a proper look-out by sight and hearing as well as by all available means......**, so the fact that a lookout failed to sight another vessel which would have been visible had he looked, does not exempt a vessel from complying with the Rules of **Section II**.

Summary of Rule 11
– Application of Part B Section II
– Conduct of Vessels in sight of one another.

Rules 12 to 18 of the Steering and Sailing Rules apply only when one vessel can actually see the other. If the other vessel can be detected only by radar, and cannot be seen visually, then Rule 19 applies. A vessel is not exempt from complying with these Rules just because a poor look-out failed to sight the other vessel.

Rule 12. Sailing vessels

> a. When two sailing vessels are approaching one another, so as to involve risk of collision, one of them shall keep out of the way of the other as follows:
> i. when each has the wind on a different side, the vessel which has the wind on the port side shall keep out of the way of the other;
> ii. when both have the wind on the same side, the vessel which is to windward shall keep out of the way of the vessel which is to leeward;
> iii. if a vessel with the wind on the port side sees a vessel to windward and cannot determine with certainty whether the other vessel has the wind on the port or starboard side, she shall keep out of the way of the other.

A sailing vessel on starboard tack, i.e. it has the wind coming over the starboard side, has right of way over a sailing vessel on port tack. (The wind is on the **right**, the boat has the **right** of way). The vessel on port tack **must keep out of the way** of the other

If two sailing vessels are on the same tack, then the vessel to windward must **keep out of the way** of the other. (The windward boat keeps clear.)

A sailing vessel on port tack, which sees another sailing vessel to windward, but cannot see which tack it is on, must assume it is on starboard tack, and so **keep out of the way**. This situation is most likely to arise at night, when it is impossible to see the sails, but it could happen by day,

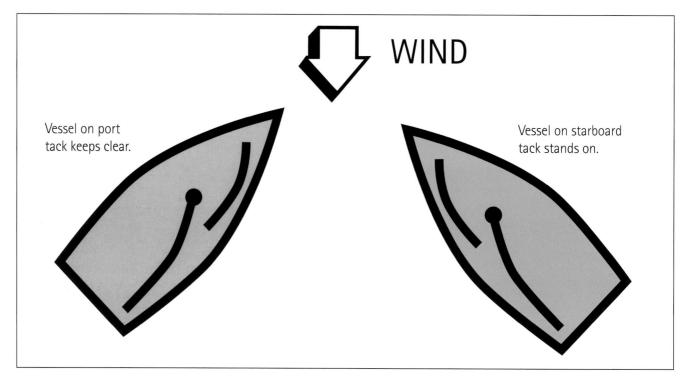

Fig 12.1 Vessel on port tack keeps clear of vessel on starboard tack.

when the nature of the sails themselves make it difficult to see on which tack it is sailing.

> b.   For the purposes of this Rule the windward side shall be deemed to be the side opposite to that on which the mainsail is carried or, in the case of a square-rigged vessel, the side opposite to that on which the largest fore-and-aft sail is carried.

This paragraph helps to define on which tack a vessel may be. Remember that, under the previous paragraph, if there is any doubt about which tack the other vessel is on, then it must be assumed to be on starboard tack.

We shall see in Rule 13 that an overtaking vessel must always keep clear of the vessel that it is overtaking. So a sailing vessel, which is approaching another vessel from more than 22.5° abaft her beam, (the definition of overtaking), must keep clear of the overtaken vessel. This applies regardless of which vessel is on which tack, in the case of a sailing vessel overtaking another sailing vessel. If a sailing vessel is overtaking a power-driven vessel, then the sailing vessel must keep clear, even though under other circumstances, a power-driven vessel would be expected to keep out of the way of a sailing vessel.

There are several other circumstances when sailing

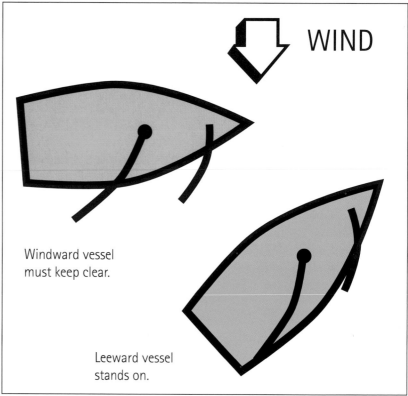

Fig 12.2 Vessels on the same tack – vessel to windward keeps clear of vessel to leeward.

vessels must keep out of the way of power-driven vessels. We shall see, when we come to **Rule 18**, (the "pecking order" between vessels), that sailing vessels must keep out of the way of vessels not under command, vessels restricted in their ability to manoeuvre, and vessels engaged in fishing. We also saw in **Rules 9 and 10** that sailing vessels must not impede the passage of vessels which can navigate only in a narrow channel or fairway, or which are navigating in a traffic separation lane.

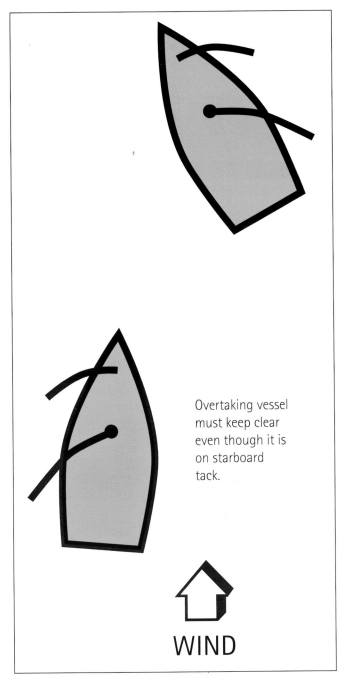

Overtaking vessel must keep clear even though it is on starboard tack.

WIND

Fig 12.3 Sailing vessel overtaking another sailing vessel must keep clear, even if the overtaking vessel is on starboard tack and the other is on port tack.

If a sailing vessel is using her sails, but also has an engine running in gear, then Rule 25 stipulates that it must display a cone, point-downwards. Such a vessel is no longer classified as a sailing vessel, but is considered to be a power-driven vessel, and loses the privileges of a sailing vessel.

Summary of Rule 12 – Sailing vessels.

1. *When sailing vessels meet on opposite tacks, the vessel on port tack must keep clear. (The vessel with the wind on the* **right** *i.e. is on starboard tack, has* **right** *of way)*
   If on the same tack, then the windward vessel must keep clear.

If there is doubt as to which tack the other vessel is on, it must be assumed to be on starboard tack.

2. *Remember that if a sailing vessel is overtaking another vessel, power or sail, it must keep clear – Rule 13. Also a sailing vessel must keep clear of vessels not under command, restricted in their ability to manoeuvre and vessels engaged in fishing – Rule 18, and they must not impede the passage of vessels which can only navigate in a narrow channel or fairway – Rule 9, or are navigating in a traffic separation lane- Rule 10.*

3. *A sailing vessel running its engine in gear is no longer considered to be a sailing vessel, and it must show a cone point-downwards in the rigging, to indicate that it is motor-sailing (Rule 25).*

Rule 13. Overtaking

> a.   Notwithstanding anything contained in the Rules of Part B, Sections I and II any vessel overtaking any other shall keep out of the way of the vessel being overtaken.

Part B of the Rules are the Steering and Sailing Rules. **Section I** includes Rules 4 to 10, and they apply in all conditions of visibility. **Section II** are Rules 11 to 18, which apply only when vessels are in sight of one another.

The Rule makes it quite clear that regardless of other rules **in Section B**, under all circumstances, an overtaking vessel keeps clear of the vessel it is overtaking.

If a sailing vessel is overtaking another sailing vessel, it does not matter which tack which vessel is on, **Rule 13** takes precedence over **Rule 12**, and the overtaking vessel must keep clear.

Similarly, if a sailing vessel is overtaking a power-driven vessel, **Rule 13** takes precedence over **Rule 18**, which says that a power-driven vessel keeps out of the way of a sailing vessel. The overtaking sailing vessel must keep out of the way of the power-driven vessel which it is overtaking.

This even applies to vessels classed as restricted in their ability to manoeuvre. If they are overtaking another vessel, they must keep clear. If they have difficulty in altering course, they can probably keep clear by slowing down.

Rule 9, the Narrow Channel Rule, stated in **paragraph c.** that even after making the overtaking signals and receiving the acknowledgement, an overtaking vessel must still comply with **Rule 13**, and keep clear of the vessel it is overtaking.

So no ifs, ands or buts. An overtaking vessel must keep out of the way of any vessel that is being overtaken.

> b.   A vessel shall be deemed to be overtaking when coming up with another vessel from a direction more than 22.5 degrees abaft her beam, that is, in such a

> position with reference to the vessel she is overtaking, that at night she would be able to see only the stern light of that vessel but neither of her sidelights.

When a vessel approaches another from more than 22.5° abaft the beam, she is deemed to be overtaking. 22.5° abaft the beam is the cut-off point for the masthead lights of a power-driven vessel, and the sidelights and stern lights for all vessels. (**Rule 21** covers arcs of visibility of lights.)

At night, the navigation lights should make it fairly obvious if there is an overtaking situation. If the stern light is visible, and the side lights and masthead lights are not, then it is an overtaking situation. If the side lights and masthead lights are visible, then it is not an overtaking situation. It is a crossing situation, and **Rule 15** would apply.

> c.   When a vessel is in any doubt as to whether she is overtaking another, she shall assume that this is the case and act accordingly.

During the day, when the navigation lights are not visible, it can be more difficult to determine the exact angle of approach. When approaching another vessel just slightly abaft the beam, it may be difficult to judge the exact angle of approach. If there is any doubt, then it must be assumed that there is an overtaking situation, and the overtaking vessel must keep out of the way of the other vessel.

> d.   Any subsequent alteration of the bearing between the two vessels shall not make the overtaking vessel a crossing vessel within the meaning of these Rules or relieve her of the duty of keeping clear of the overtaken vessel until she is finally past and clear.

When an overtaking vessel approaches another vessel from more than 22.5° abaft the beam, she is the overtaking vessel, and as such, she must keep clear. As she overtakes the other vessel, obviously the bearing changes, and eventually she will find herself ahead of the other vessel. However, she cannot alter course, and become a crossing vessel, claiming the right of way. For example, if a vessel overtakes another on her starboard side, and then altered course to port across the bows of the overtaken vessel, the overtaken vessel would be bound under **Rule 15** to keep out of the way, since the overtaking vessel is now on her starboard bow. This is obviously unsatisfactory, so this part of the Rule makes it plain that the obligation of the overtaking vessel to keep out of the way of the overtaken vessel continues <u>until it is past and clear</u> of the other vessel. The overtaking vessel is expressly forbidden to make an overtaking situation into a crossing situation.

The only exception would be if one vessel overtook another at a considerable distance, in the order of several miles. They could well be in sight of each other, but if the distance was sufficiently large, it would not be deemed that there was any risk of collision. If the overtaking vessel subsequently altered course, and approached the other vessel on a bearing of less than 22.5° abaft the beam, then the normal crossing Rules would apply. It must be stressed though that this situation would only apply if there were a gap of several miles between the vessels, so that the overtaken vessel would have plenty of time to plot the other vessel, assess the situation, and respond as necessary.

The overtaking vessel is required to **keep out of the way** of the overtaken vessel, and if there is a risk of collision, then under **Rule 8. a.** she must **take positive and early action**, and under **Rule 8. d.**, she is required **to pass at a safe distance**. There is nothing in the Rules to say that the overtaking vessel cannot pass ahead of the overtaken vessel, but it must be done at a safe distance. Generally it is safer for the overtaking vessel to slow down, and pass behind the other vessel, but in any event, her actions must be **positive**, and **made in ample time**, so the overtaken vessel is left in no doubt as to the intentions of the overtaking vessel.

In a narrow channel, the overtaking vessel must assess if it is safe to overtake, before beginning the overtaking manoeuvre. If it requires the co-operation of the other vessel, the overtaking vessel must signal its intention:

- Two prolonged and a short blast – I intend to overtake you on your starboard side.
- Two prolonged and two short blasts – I intend to overtake you on your port side.

If the vessel about to be overtaken agrees, she sounds:
- Prolonged, short, prolonged, short blasts (Morse code C - · - ·).

If she disagrees, she sounds:
- At least five short and rapid blasts.

The responsibility for keeping clear still rests with the overtaking vessel, even after the other vessel has signalled its agreement.

In assessing if it is safe to pass, the overtaking vessel must take into consideration any likely interaction between the two vessels as they pass close together, the possibility of interaction between the other vessel and the bank, if it has to pass close to the bank to permit the overtaking, and also the effect of the vessel's wake on the overtaken vessel. This may be considerable, if the overtaken vessel is small, and is navigating in shallow water to permit the other vessel to pass. Generally all of these effects will be minimised if the overtaking vessel slows to a speed just a little faster than the overtaken vessel. The responsibility rests with the overtaking vessel.

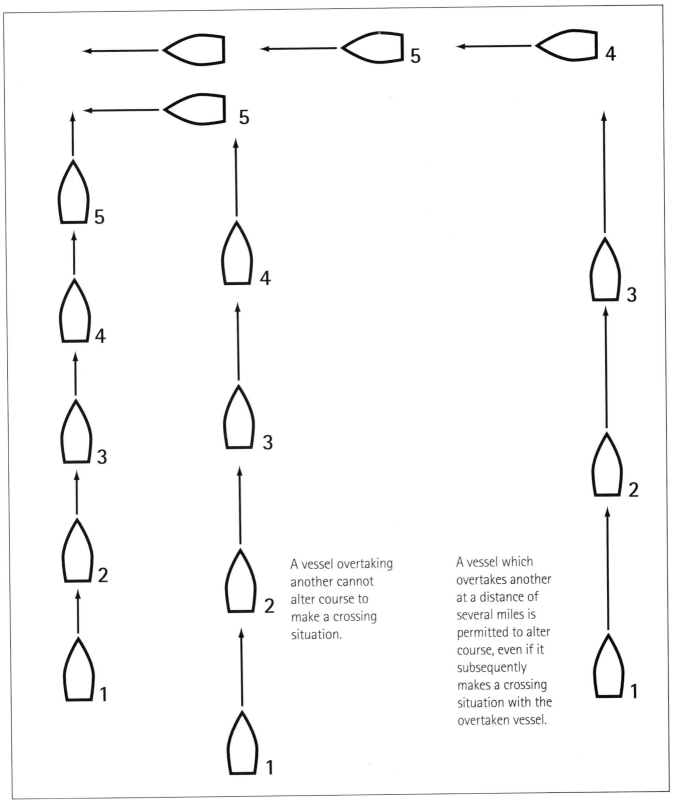

A vessel overtaking another cannot alter course to make a crossing situation.

A vessel which overtakes another at a distance of several miles is permitted to alter course, even if it subsequently makes a crossing situation with the overtaken vessel.

Fig 13.1 A vessel overtaking cannot alter course to make a crossing situation, unless the overtaking was completed at a distance of several miles.

Summary of Rule 13 – Overtaking

1. A vessel is deemed to be overtaking if it approaches another vessel more than 22.5° abaft her beam, that is within the arc of the stern light of the other vessel. If there is any doubt that an overtaking situation exists, then it must be assumed that it does exist.

2. An overtaking vessel must <u>always</u> keep out of the way of an overtaken vessel. The responsibility to keep clear continues until the overtaking vessel is past and clear. It cannot turn an overtaking situation into a crossing situation, and expect to have right of way.

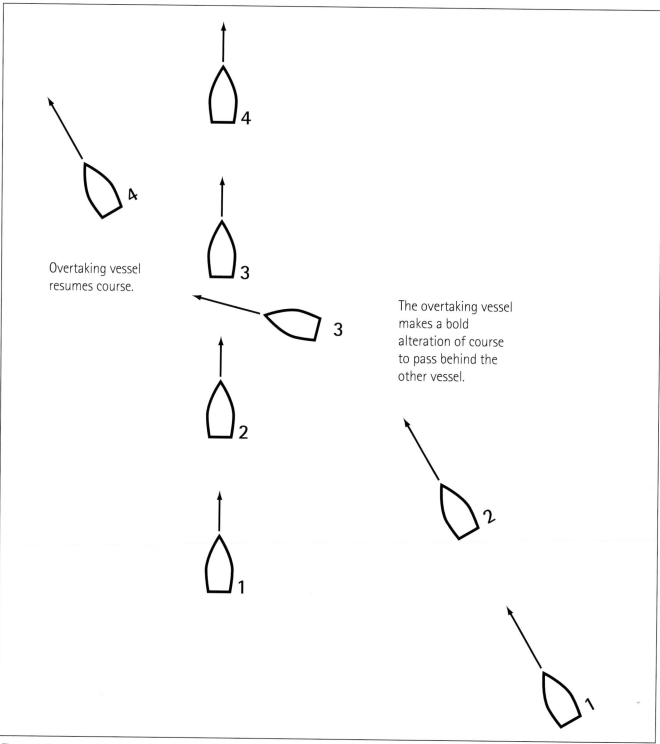

Overtaking vessel
resumes course.

The overtaking vessel
makes a bold
alteration of course
to pass behind the
other vessel.

Fig 13.2 The overtaking vessel makes a positive alteration of course to pass behind the other vessel.

Rule 14. Head-on Situation

a.   When two power-driven vessels are meeting on reciprocal or nearly reciprocal courses so as to involve risk of collision each shall alter her course to starboard so that each shall pass on the port side of the other.

When two power-driven vessels are meeting almost head on, the responsibility to keep clear is equally shared. Both vessels are obliged to alter course to starboard, so the two vessels pass port-to-port.

b.   Such a situation shall be deemed to exist when a vessel sees the other ahead or nearly ahead and by night she could see the masthead lights of the other in a line or nearly in a line and/or both sidelights and by day she observes the corresponding aspect of the other vessel.

It is not intended for **Rule 14** to apply when only one sidelight of the approaching vessel is visible. In **Annex I, Section 9**, it is stipulated that the cut-off point for the light from the port and starboard navigation lights must be between 1° and 3° outside of the prescribed arc. This results in each sidelight being visible from between 1° and 3° on the opposite bow, which means that through an arc of 2° to 6°, both sidelights should be seen at the same time. This eliminates the possibility of a dark sector, where neither sidelight could be seen from ahead.

At night, if both sidelights can be seen at the same time, then **Rule 14** applies. If only one light is visible, then it does not. By day, if the approaching vessel appears to be head-on, or very nearly so, then **Rule 14** applies.

> c. When a vessel is in any doubt as to whether such a situation exists she shall assume that it does exist and act accordingly.

A potentially dangerous situation can arise if two vessels approach on reciprocal courses which would lead them to pass close to each other, starboard-to-starboard. A collision situation could arise if one vessel chose to alter course to port, to increase the distance of the starboard-to-

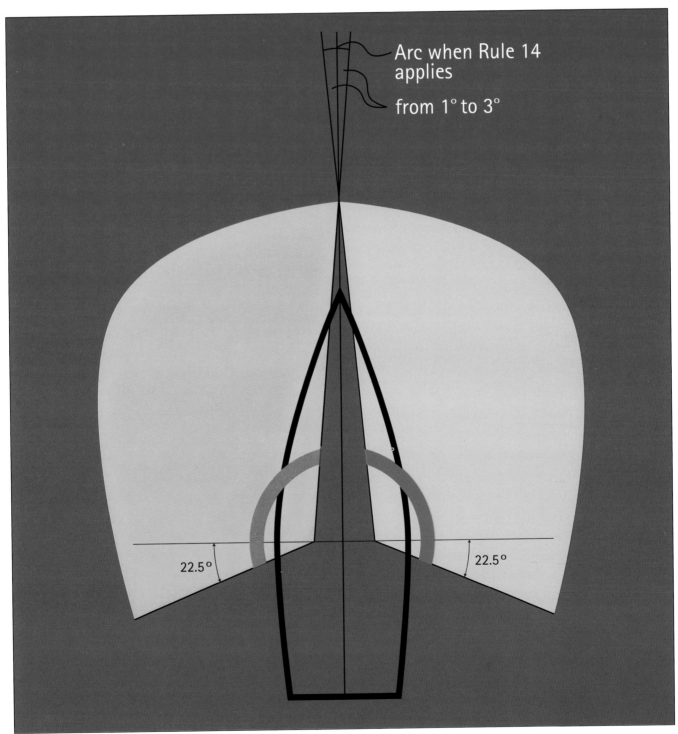

Arc when Rule 14 applies

from 1° to 3°

22.5°   22.5°

Figure 14.1 Arcs of visibility of the port and starboard navigation lights.

starboard passing, while the other vessel decided that **Rule 14** applied, and altered to starboard, trying to pass port-to-port.

When two vessels are on course to pass starboard-to-starboard, if it is felt necessary to increase the passing distance, then it must be considered that there is some risk of collision. If it were thought that there was no risk of collision, it should not have been necessary to increase the passing distance.

If there is a risk of collision, then the vessels must act according to the Rules. This paragraph is telling us that if there is any doubt that there is a head-on situation, then we must assume that there is, and that <u>each vessel</u> **shall** (note it says <u>shall</u>, not "may", or "if you feel like it",) alter **course to starboard**, to pass the other vessel port-to-port.

Remember that **Rule 8** told us that any action we take to avoid a collision should be **positive**, and **made in ample time**. Early, positive actions are more likely to let the other vessel understand your intentions, than would a series of small, last-minute manoeuvres.

Summary of Rule 14 – Head-on Situation.

1. *If two power-driven vessels meet head-on, or nearly head-on, and there is a risk of collision, then both vessels* **shall** *alter course to starboard.*
2. *If there is any doubt whether it is a "head-on" situation, or a "crossing" situation, then it must be assumed to be head-on, and both vessels* **shall** *alter course to starboard.*

(Alterations to port should be avoided as far as possible, because if the other vessel correctly alters to starboard, a collision situation is likely to arise.)

Rule 15. Crossing Situation

> When two power-driven vessels are crossing so as to involve risk of collision, the vessel which has the other on her own starboard side shall keep out of the way and shall, if the circumstances of the case admit, avoid crossing ahead of the other vessel.

We have seen that if one vessel approaches another from more than 22.5° abaft the beam, then the vessel is deemed to be overtaking, and it must keep out of the way – **Rule 13**. If two vessels approach head-on, or nearly head-on, then both vessels are required to alter course to starboard – **Rule 14**. **Rule 15** deals with two power-driven vessels approaching at <u>any other angle</u> – i.e. from about 3° off either bow, to 22.5° abaft either beam.

A vessel which has another on her starboard side **shall** keep out of the way of the other. This vessel is termed the give-way vessel. At night, the give-way vessel will see the red navigation light of the other vessel, (except under rare conditions such as when navigating in a strong current). To help remember which vessel must give way, the red light can be thought of as a stop signal. The vessel which sees the red light must "stop", or alter course to give way.

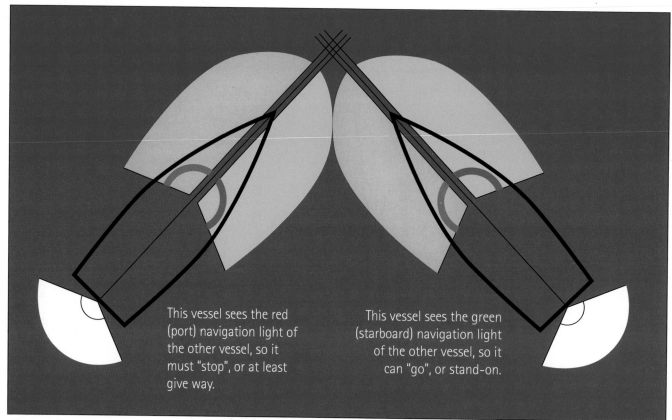

This vessel sees the red (port) navigation light of the other vessel, so it must "stop", or at least give way.

This vessel sees the green (starboard) navigation light of the other vessel, so it can "go", or stand-on.

Fig 15.1 Two vessels in a crossing situation, and the arcs of visibility of their navigation lights.

The other vessel, which is termed the stand-on vessel, will see the green starboard light of the give-way vessel. This can be thought of as the signal to go, or at least to proceed with caution!

The Rule says that the give-way vessel must try to avoid passing ahead of the stand-on vessel. This effectively means that as in **Rule 14** – the Head-on Rule, the give-way vessel is being told to alter course to starboard, to go behind the other vessel, rather than alter to port, to cross the bows of the stand-on vessel.

The restriction on passing ahead only applies when there is deemed to be a risk of collision. If two vessels are crossing at a distance of several miles, or when the bearing of one vessel from the other is changing rapidly, and there is no risk of collision, then it is permitted for the vessel which has the other vessel on its starboard bow to cross ahead. But if there is any risk of collision, then the give-way vessel must alter course to starboard, and pass astern of the other vessel, or of course it may slow down or stop, to allow the stand-on vessel to pass ahead.

We should again remember that **Rule 8** told us that any actions we take to avoid a collision must be **positive**, and **made in ample time**. As always, positive action, taken early, lets the other vessel understand your intentions.

There are a number of circumstances when **Rule 15** does not apply:

Rule 9 (**N**ine for **N**arrow Channels) states that **a vessel shall not cross a narrow channel or fairway if such crossing impedes the passage of a vessel which can safely navigate only in such channel or fairway**. So a vessel wanting to cross a narrow channel cannot use **Rule 15** to make a vessel in the channel give way. It must wait for a suitable opportunity, when it can cross without impeding any vessel which cannot navigate outside of the channel.

Rule 10 (**T**en for **T**raffic Separation Schemes) states that when crossing a traffic separation scheme, a **vessel of less than 20 metres in length or a sailing vessel shall not impede the passage of a power-driven vessel following a traffic lane**. So neither a small vessel, nor a sailing vessel can use **Rule 15** to help it cross a busy traffic separation lane. As in the narrow channel situation, they must await a suitable opportunity before crossing (remembering to cross on a <u>heading</u> at right angles to the general flow of the traffic), so they can cross without impeding the passage of a power-driven vessel following the lane. For power-driven vessels over 20 metres crossing a traffic lane (again on a <u>heading</u> at right angles to the general flow of traffic), then **Rule 15** does apply – the vessels navigating in the traffic lane gain no special privileges.

If a power-driven vessel sees a "hampered vessel" crossing on her port bow, then **Rule 18** – Responsibilities Between Vessels (or what I like to call the "pecking order of vessels") comes into play. We will look at it in more detail

when we get to **Rule 18**, but basically a power-driven vessel must keep out of the way of:

- vessels not under command;
- vessels restricted in their ability to manoeuvre;
- vessels engaged in fishing;
- sailing vessels.

When a power-driven vessel meets any of the above vessels in a crossing situation, then **Rule 18** (Pecking Order) takes precedence over **Rule 15** (Crossing Rule), and the power-driven vessel must keep clear.

A vessel towing, unless it is displaying the signals indicating that it is restricted in its ability to manoeuvre, has no special right-of-way privileges. It is treated as any other power-driven vessel, and so **Rule 15** would apply in a crossing situation. However, when we look at **Rule 17** – Actions of Stand-on Vessels (**S**eventeen for **S**tand-on vessels), we will see that there are fairly specific periods when the stand-on vessel is allowed to alter course or speed, must maintain her course and speed, and must alter course or speed.

If a power-driven vessel sees, for example, a tug and tow crossing from her port bow, the stand-on vessel <u>may</u> alter course or speed when distances are such that there is no risk of collision. As soon as the vessels are close enough that there could be deemed to be a risk of collision, then the stand-on vessel must hold her course and speed. If it becomes apparent that the give-way vessel is not taking sufficient action, or cannot keep out of the way, then the stand-on vessel <u>may</u> alter course or speed. The stand-on vessel <u>must</u> alter course or speed if the vessels get close enough that the give-way vessel cannot avoid collision by her efforts alone. In the case of the crossing tug and tow, the stand-on vessel may well elect to take early action under **Rule 17**, if it becomes apparent that the tug may be having some difficulty altering her course. Once again though, the stand-on vessel, seeing a tug and tow on her port bow, should avoid altering course to port, to go behind the tug and tow, because there is a good possibility that the tug is trying to alter course to starboard, and this could result in a collision situation. However, it may be equally dangerous to pass close ahead of the tug, so possibly the best course of action would be to slow down, and let the tug pass ahead.

Never forget **Rule 8** (Actions to Avoid Collisions), and take **positive action**, in **ample time**, so the tug knows exactly what your intentions are. There is probably a good case for calling the tug on the VHF - there should be little problem in identifying each other, and mutually agree a course of action.

A vessel which is constrained by her draught, even if she is displaying the correct signals, is not exempt from complying with **Rule 15**. Such a vessel is expected to keep out of the way of a power-driven vessel which is crossing on her starboard bow, so as to involve a risk of collision. However, **Rule 18** (the "pecking order"), states that **any vessel, other than a vessel not under command or restricted in her ability to manoeuvre shall, if the circumstances of the case admit, avoid impeding the passage of a vessel constrained by her draught, exhibiting the signals in Rule 28.** Note that to be classed as constrained by her draught, the vessel must show the appropriate signals of three red lights in a row at night, or a cylinder by day.

Once again, always remember **Rule 8** (Action to Avoid a Collision), which says that whatever action you take to avoid a collision must be **positive** and taken in **ample time**. Also, do not forget **Rule 17** (Stand-on vessels) which says that the stand-on vessel <u>may</u> take action when it becomes apparent that the other vessel is not taking action, or cannot take sufficient action, and <u>must</u> take action when the give-way vessel cannot avoid collision by her actions alone. Although you might have right-of-way over a large vessel, which is constrained by her draught, you must be prepared to take avoiding action in ample time, if she is unable to avoid a risk of collision by her own efforts.

A vessel which is stopped, that is, not making way through the water (perhaps waiting for a pilot, or for a tide to enter a port), is still considered to be underway. **Rule 2** stated that any vessel which **is not at anchor, made fast to the shore, or aground** is considered to be underway.

Any vessel which is underway, (unless she is not under command, or restricted in her ability to manoeuvre, and showing the appropriate signals), is expected to keep out of the way of any vessel approaching on the starboard side between ahead and 22.5° abaft the starboard beam. A vessel does not lose this responsibility, just because she is not making way. Such a vessel must maintain a lookout at all times (**Rule 5**), and have her engines ready to manoeuvre, to take avoiding action.

Summary of Rule 15 – the Crossing Rule.

1. *If two power-driven vessels are crossing, which means approaching from near ahead to 22.5° abaft either beam, then the vessel which has the other on her starboard side must keep clear. (The give-way vessel will usually see the red navigation light of the stand-on vessel, telling it to "stop", or alter course, and the stand-on vessel will usually see the green navigation light of the give-way vessel, telling it keep going.)*

2. *The give-way vessel should try not to cross ahead of the stand-on vessel, and should avoid altering course to port whenever possible.*

3. *In narrow channels and traffic lanes, sailing vessels, fishing vessels or power-driven vessels under 20 metres cannot use Rule 15 to cross, as Rule 9 and Rule 10 state that such vessels when crossing must not impede the passage of vessels within the channel or lane.*

4. *Rule 18 (the Pecking Order) gives precedence to hampered vessels in a crossing situation.*

5. *Being stopped in the water does not give a vessel any exemption from complying with Rule 15.*

Rule 16. Action by Give-Way Vessel

> Every vessel which is directed to keep out of the way of another vessel shall, so far as possible, take early and substantial action to keep well clear.

There are four Rules which direct one vessel to **keep out of the way** of another vessel. They are:

- **Rule 12** – Sailing Vessels.
- **Rule 13** – Overtaking Situations.
- **Rule 15** – Crossing Situations.
- **Rule 18** – Responsibilities between Vessels, (The "Pecking Order").

In each case, one vessel is directed to **keep out of the way** of another vessel. This vessel is termed the **give-way vessel**, and the other is the **stand-on vessel**. Rule 16 states that the **give-way vessel** must **take early and substantial action to keep well clear**, when any one of these four Rules apply.

Rule 8 told us how we must take action to avoid a collision. The first paragraph said that **Any action taken to avoid a collision shall, if the circumstances of the case admit, be positive, made in ample time and with due regard to the observance of good seamanship. Rule 8** is in **Section I**, and so applies in <u>all conditions of visibility.</u>

Rule 16 is in **Section II**, so it applies only when vessels are <u>in sight of one another</u>. Although the words are different, the message is the same. Whether you are manoeuvring to keep clear of another vessel, or to avoid a risk of collision, take the action soon, and make the action big enough to make your intentions obvious to the other vessel.

Rule 16 states that the give-way vessel must **keep well clear. Rule 8** said that the actions had to result in passing at a **safe distance**. Again, the words are different, but the message is the same – when keeping clear of another vessel, do not cut it close, but keep a safe distance away.

Rule 8 also reminded us that the give-way vessel can slow down or even stop, to give more time to assess the situation, and must monitor the effectiveness of any action until the other vessel is past and clear. This is obviously equally applicable under **Rule 16**.

If the give-way vessel is compelled to alter course to avoid a collision, and the vessels are in sight of each other, then **Rule 34** (Manoeuvring and Warning Signals), states that she <u>must</u> sound the appropriate signal on the whistle:

- One short blast – I am altering course to starboard;

- Two short blasts – I am altering course to port.

These <u>may</u> be supplemented with a light signal:

- One flash – I am altering course to starboard;
- Two flashes – I am altering course to port.

If the give-way vessel decides to slow down, and engages astern propulsion, then she <u>must</u> sound three short blasts, which <u>may</u> be supplemented with three flashes of a light signal.

Summary of Rule 16 – Action by Give-way Vessel.

1. *A vessel which is required to keep out of the way of another vessel <u>must</u> take* **early and substantial action** *to keep* **well clear**.
2. *Rules 12 (Sailing vessels), 13 (Overtaking situations), 15 (Crossing situations) and 18 (Responsibilities Between Vessels), all direct one vessel to* **keep out of the way** *of another vessel. Rule 16 (Action by Give-way vessel), and the four "Keep-out-of-the-way Rules" apply only when the vessels are in sight of one another.*
3. *If the give-way vessel has to alter course to avoid a collision, she <u>must</u> sound the appropriate signals on the whistle (One blast – altering to starboard, Two blasts – altering to port) Rule 34.*

Rule 17. Action by Stand-on Vessel

> a.i.   Where one of two vessels is to keep out of the way, the other shall keep her course and speed. .

The vessel which is directed to **keep out of the way** of another vessel is called the **give-way vessel**. The other vessel is the **stand-on vessel**.

As we just saw in Rule 16, there are four Rules which direct one vessel to **keep out of the way** of another. These Rules are:

- **Rule 12** – Sailing Vessels.
- **Rule 13** – Overtaking Situations.
- **Rule 15** – Crossing Situations.
- **Rule 18** – Responsibilities between Vessels (The "Pecking Order").

Rule 17, and the above four Rules, apply only when one vessel can see the other.

If another vessel is detected by radar, but cannot be sighted visually, we will see in **Rule 19** that there is no stand-on vessel. Both vessels will be expected to manoeuvre so as to avoid a risk of collision developing.

If a vessel is sighted at long range (what constitutes "long range" depends on the circumstances and the manoeuvrability of the vessels concerned, but is likely to be several miles), even if the bearing of the other vessel is

constant, there would not be deemed to be any risk of collision, because the vessels are so far apart. Until the vessels get closer together, none of these five Rules apply. Both vessels are free to manoeuvre as they please, until such time as the vessels get close enough for it to be considered that there is a risk of collision. At that moment, the stand-on vessel must hold her course and speed, until section ii of the Rule becomes a factor.

> ii.   The latter (stand-on) vessel may however take action to avoid collision by her manoeuvre alone, as soon as it becomes apparent to her that the vessel required to keep out of the way is not taking appropriate action in compliance with these Rules.

The stand-on vessel <u>may</u> take action when she feels that the give-way vessel is not taking action early enough, or that the action is not sufficient to ensure passing at a safe distance. She is not legally required to take action at this point, but <u>may</u> take action. We will see in the next paragraph of the Rule that the stand-on vessel <u>must</u> take action when the two vessels get so close that collision cannot be avoided by the action of the give-way vessel alone. That point is obviously very difficult to judge, and if just slightly misjudged, could well end up in a collision between the two vessels. By taking action at this earlier stage, the risk of collision is substantially reduced.

When it becomes apparent that the give-way vessel is not taking appropriate action, the first action by the stand-on vessel would be to sound the "Wake Up Signal" prescribed in **Rule 34 d**. This is at least five short and rapid blasts on the whistle, which <u>may</u> be supplemented with a light signal of five short and rapid flashes.

If the give-way vessel still does not appear to be taking appropriate action, and the stand-on vessel decides to alter her course or speed, then, as we will see, under **Rule 34**, she <u>must</u> signal her intention to alter course by the appropriate signals on the whistle:

- One short blast – I am altering my course to starboard;
- Two short blasts – I am altering my course to port.

These signals <u>may</u> be supplemented with light signals:

- One flash – I am altering my course to starboard;
- Two flashes – I am altering my course to port.

If the stand-on vessel decides to slow down, and engages astern propulsion, then she <u>must</u> sound three short blasts, which <u>may</u> be supplemented with three flashes.

As we saw in **Rule 16**, and will see again in **Rule 34**, provided that the vessels are in sight, (which they must be, for **Rule 17** to apply) the give-way vessel is also obliged to give the appropriate sound signals, if she alters course to avoid a risk of collision.

> b.   When, from any cause, the vessel required to keep her course and speed finds herself so close that collision cannot be avoided by the action of the give-way vessel alone, she shall take such action as will best aid to avoid collision.

> c.   A power-driven vessel which takes action in a crossing situation in accordance with sub-paragraph (a) (ii) of this Rule to avoid collision with another power-driven vessel, shall if the circumstances of the case admit, not alter course to port for a vessel on her own port side.

When the give-way vessel cannot avoid a collision by her manoeuvres alone, then the stand-on vessel must act – the Rule says **shall**, not may. The stand-on vessel is directed to act in the way which is most likely to avoid a collision – this may be to alter course, it may be to alter speed, or it could well be both. Remember that changing speed requires more time to take effect, and more time for it to become apparent to the other vessel than does a change of course.

If the stand-on vessel decides to alter speed, the normal reaction is to slow down. However, if, at the last moment, the give-way vessel alters course to starboard, and attempts to go astern of the stand-on vessel, the act of the stand-on vessel slowing down could make the situation worse. The stand-on vessel must continue to monitor and assess the situation, and it could be that an increase in speed may be needed, to save the situation.

If a collision still results, then the stand-on vessel is likely to be held at least partially to blame for the collision, because although she is obliged to take action only when a collision cannot be avoided by the action of the give-way vessel alone, she was permitted to take action sooner. She could have altered course and/or speed as soon as it became apparent that the give-way vessel was not taking appropriate action. The stand-on vessel is expected to monitor and continually assess the situation, and not stand-on blindly.

The exact moment where a **collision cannot be avoided by the action of the give-way vessel alone** is obviously very hard to judge. It depends on the size, speed and manoeuvrability of the vessels, but in a crossing situation the distance between a vessel and the point of impact is likely to be at least four or five times the length of the vessel. It could be much greater than this if the give-way vessel is not very manoeuvrable, and the stand-on vessel is approaching at high speed.

We saw in paragraph **a. ii.** that the stand-on vessel is allowed to take action **as soon as it becomes apparent to her**, that the give-way vessel is not taking action, or is not taking sufficient action. The stand-on vessel should never let a give-way vessel get so close that "a collision cannot be avoided by the action of the give-way vessel alone", without initiating some action of her own. In a crossing situation in the open-sea, the stand-on vessel should be initiating an alteration of course and/or speed when the give-way vessel is still at least twelve to fifteen vessel lengths away, if it is not obvious that the give-way vessel has initiated a suitable action.

Note that it says that this paragraph only applies to **Section a. ii.**, which says that the stand-on vessel <u>may</u> take action to avoid a collision as soon as it becomes apparent to her that the give-way vessel is not taking suitable action, so by inference, it is not intended to apply to **paragraph b.**, which says that the give-way vessel <u>must</u> take action if the vessels get so close that the give-way vessel cannot avoid collision by her action alone. We will see that this distinction could be important.

In a crossing situation, **Rule 15** told us that the give-way vessel should try to avoid crossing the bows of the stand-on vessel. If it is a crossing situation, the give-way vessel must be on the port bow of the stand-on vessel. In such a situation, if the stand-on vessel decided that it should take action, because the give-way vessel does not appear to be taking the appropriate action, and if the stand-on vessel were to alter to port, and it then turned out that the give-way vessel had altered to starboard, as it should, to try to go behind the stand-on vessel, a collision could result. Paragraph **c.** is telling us that we should try to not alter course to port for a vessel on our port side, so we do not fall into this trap.

The best options for the stand-on vessel would be to alter speed, or alter course to starboard. If she does alter course to starboard, she is <u>required</u> by **Rule 34** to sound one short blast on the whistle, which <u>may</u> be supplemented with a light signal. If she slows down, and needs to engage astern propulsion, then she <u>must</u> sound three short blasts, which <u>may</u> be supplemented with a light signal.

If the give-way vessel makes an early and substantial alteration of course, and signifies this with the appropriate signal, there will be little chance for confusion. However, a small alteration, and no signal, may lead the stand-on vessel to believe that no action has been initiated.

If the situation has deteriorated to the point where collision cannot be avoided by the action of the give-way vessel alone, then the restriction of not trying to avoid turns to port does not apply, and the stand-on vessel must manoeuvre so as to best avoid a collision. If a collision is inevitable, then the stand-on vessel must manoeuvre so as to minimise damage. Under these circumstances, a turn to port may well be the best solution, (as well as trying to reduce speed). If one vessel is likely to strike the other abaft of amidships, then a turn to port could reduce the collision to a glancing blow, whereas a turn to starboard could result in hitting the other vessel amidships.

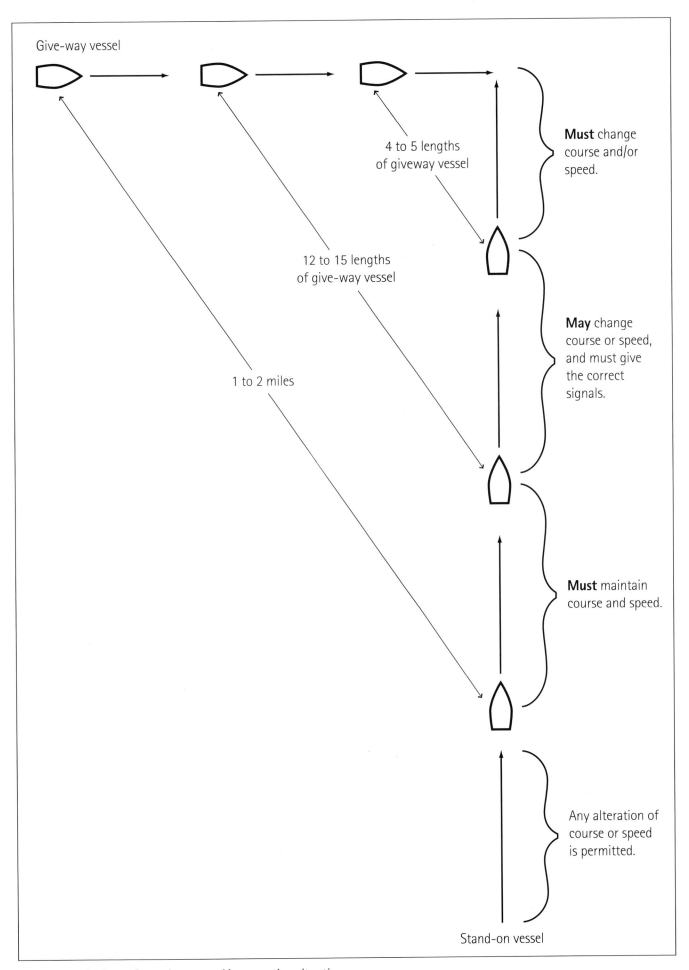

Give-way vessel

Must change course and/or speed.

4 to 5 lengths of giveway vessel

12 to 15 lengths of give-way vessel

May change course or speed, and must give the correct signals.

1 to 2 miles

Must maintain course and speed.

Any alteration of course or speed is permitted.

Stand-on vessel

Figure 17.1 Actions of stand-on vessel in a crossing situation.

45

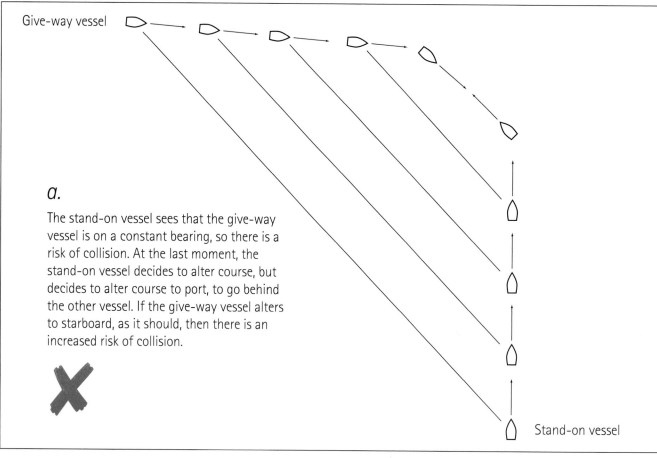

Give-way vessel

a.

The stand-on vessel sees that the give-way vessel is on a constant bearing, so there is a risk of collision. At the last moment, the stand-on vessel decides to alter course, but decides to alter course to port, to go behind the other vessel. If the give-way vessel alters to starboard, as it should, then there is an increased risk of collision.

Stand-on vessel

Figure 17.2 Crossing situation.
    a. the stand-on vessel altering course to port, resulting in an increased risk of collision;
    b. the stand-on vessel correctly altering course to starboard.

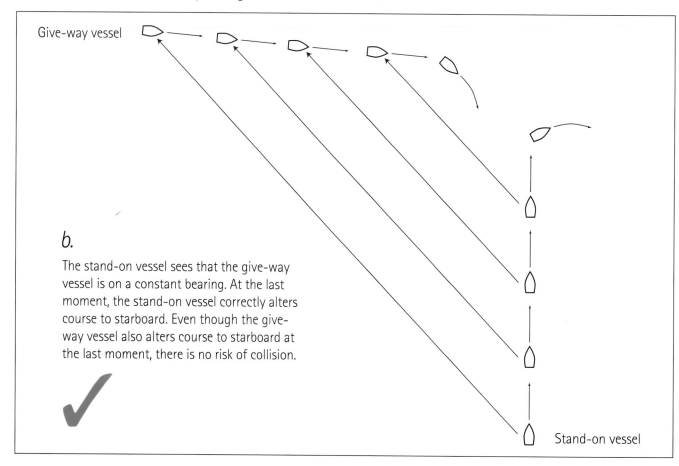

Give-way vessel

b.

The stand-on vessel sees that the give-way vessel is on a constant bearing. At the last moment, the stand-on vessel correctly alters course to starboard. Even though the give-way vessel also alters course to starboard at the last moment, there is no risk of collision.

Stand-on vessel

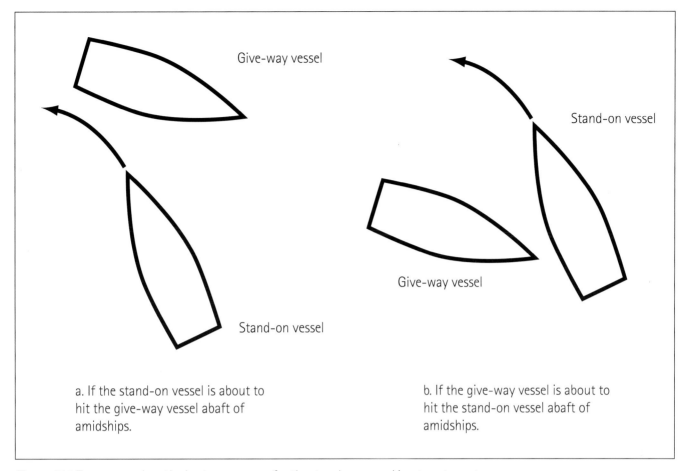

a. If the stand-on vessel is about to hit the give-way vessel abaft of amidships.

b. If the give-way vessel is about to hit the stand-on vessel abaft of amidships.

Figure 17.3 Two cases when the best manoeuvre for the stand-on vessel is a turn to port.

> d.   This Rule does not relieve the give-way vessel of her obligation to keep out of the way.

This paragraph makes it plain that the give-way vessel is not allowed to wait, in the hope that the stand-on vessel will alter course or speed to pass at a safe distance. As soon as there is a risk of collision, the give-way vessel *must* **take early and substantial action to keep well clear – Rule 16**, and once there is a risk of collision, the stand-on vessel is not allowed to take action until it is apparent that the give-way vessel is failing in her obligation **– Rule 17**.

Even if the stand-on vessel initiates a manoeuvre, in accordance with **Section a. ii.**, because she feels that the give-way vessel is not taking sufficient action, the give-way vessel is not relieved of her obligation to keep out of the way.

Summary of Rule 17 – Action by Stand-on Vessel.

1. *When two vessels are far enough away from each other, so that there is not deemed to be a risk of collision, then both vessels are free to manoeuvre as they wish.*

2. *As soon as there is thought to be a risk of collision, then the* **give-way vessel** *must* t*ake* **early and substantial action to keep well clear**, *and the* **stand-on vessel** *must* **keep her course and speed**.

3. *If it becomes apparent that the give-way vessel is either not initiating action soon enough, or sufficiently to ensure passing at a safe distance, the* **stand-on vessel may take action.** *The first action would probably be to sound the "Wake-up signal" as stipulated in Rule 34 – at least five short and rapid blasts on the whistle, which* may *be supplemented with a light signal. If that produces no result, the next action would probably be to alter course and/or speed. A power-driven vessel should try to avoid turning to port for another power-driven vessel on her port side. If the stand-on vessel alters course to starboard, she* must *sound one blast on the whistle to signify her intentions, and this* may *be supplemented with a light signal.*

4. *Even if the stand-on vessel initiates a manoeuvre, to avoid a risk of collision,* **the give-way vessel is not relieved of her obligation to keep well clear.**

5. *When the vessels are so close that collision cannot be avoided by the action of the give-way vessel alone, then the stand-on vessel* must t*ake* **such action as will best aid to avoid a collision.**

6. *If a collision is inevitable, then the stand-on vessel must manoeuvre so as to minimise damage. If it appears that one vessel will hit the other abaft of amidships, then the best course of action may well be a turn to port.*

Rule 18. Responsibilities Between Vessels

(The Pecking Order of Vessels)

> **Except where Rules 9** (Narrow channels), **10** (Traffic separations) **and 13** (Overtaking) **otherwise require:**
> a. A power-driven vessel underway shall keep out of the way of:
> i. a vessel not under command;
> ii. a vessel restricted in her ability to manoeuvre;
> iii. a vessel engaged in fishing;
> iv. a sailing vessel.

Note that this part of the Rule refers to any **power-driven vessel underway**, not just to those which are making way. A power-driven vessel which is stopped in the water, but not **at anchor, or made fast to the shore, or aground,** (**Rule 3.i.**) is obliged to keep out of the way of vessels which are not under command, restricted in their ability to manoeuvre, vessels engaged in fishing and sailing vessels just the same as if she were making way. So a vessel stopped in the water, perhaps waiting for a tide to enable it to enter a harbour, is obliged to keep watch, and to have her engines ready to manoeuvre, so as to keep out of the way of any of the stipulated vessels, or indeed of another power-driven vessel which may approach on her starboard bow.

The first sentence of the Rule reminds us that there are some exceptions, under **Rules 9, 10 and 11**.

Rule 9, (Narrow Channels), told us that a vessel of less than 20 metres in length, or a sailing vessel, shall not impede the passage of a vessel which can only navigate safely within the narrow channel or fairway, and a vessel engaged in fishing cannot impede the passage of any vessel navigating within the narrow channel or fairway.

Rule 10, (Traffic Separation Zones), stated that a vessel of less than 20 metres in length, or a sailing vessel shall not impede the safe passage of a power-driven vessel following a traffic lane, and a fishing vessel shall not impede the passage of any vessel following a traffic lane.

Rule 13, (Overtaking) stipulates that the overtaking vessel must always keep out of the way of the vessel being overtaken. This Rule applies regardless of the class of vessels involved, so a sailing vessel must keep out of the way of a power-driven vessel, if it is overtaking it.

For a vessel to be considered **not under command, Rule 3** states that there must be **some exceptional circumstance** which renders her unable to manoeuvre according to the Rules. To be treated as not under command, she must display the signals required by **Rule**

27, namely two balls in a vertical line by day, and two all-round red lights by night.

A vessel **restricted in her ability to manoeuvre** is one which by the nature of her work is unable to manoeuvre as required by the Rules, and is unable to keep out of the way of other vessels. **Rule 3** defined vessels which are classed as restricted in their ability to manoeuvre. Such vessels include those engaged in:

- Laying, servicing or picking up a navigation mark, submarine cable or pipeline;
- Dredging, surveying or underwater operations;
- Replenishment or transferring persons, provisions or cargo while underway;
- A vessel engaged in the launching or recovery of aircraft;
- Mine clearance operations;
- Towing, such as severely restricts the towing vessel and her tow in their ability to deviate from their course. A normal tug and tow is not granted any special privileges, and is considered as any other power-driven vessel.

Any vessel which is to be considered as **restricted in her ability to manoeuvre** must show the appropriate signals, as specified in **Rule 27**, namely a ball, a diamond and a ball in a vertical line by day, and by night, three all-round lights in a vertical line, red, white and red. An exception is the minesweeper, which has her own signals – three balls in a triangle by day, and three all-round green lights in a triangle by night.

For a **fishing vessel** to be considered privileged, she must be engaged in fishing with nets, lines, trawls or other fishing apparatus which restrict manoeuvrability. This does not include vessels fishing with trolling lines, or other fishing apparatus which does not restrict manoeuvrability. Once again, the proper signals must be displayed if the vessel is to be considered privileged. They are specified in **Rule 26** – by day the signal is two cones, one above the other, with their apexes touching (point-to-point), and by night, two all-round lights, one above the other. The lights are green over white for a trawler and red over white for a vessel fishing other than trawling. Additionally, a vessel which is fishing other than trawling, if it has gear extending more than 150 metres, is obliged to indicate this fact with a cone, apex up by day, or an all-round white light by night, in the direction of the gear.

Sailing vessels are not required to show any special signals, but may show two all-round lights, red over green, at night, as stipulated in **Rule 25**. If a sailing vessel uses an auxiliary motor to help drive the vessel, then she ceases to be a sailing vessel, and even if all sails remain set, she is, as far as the Rules are concerned, a power-driven vessel. We will also see that under **Rule 25** she is required to display a cone, point downwards, if she is using sails and motor, to indicate that she is not longer privileged as a sailing vessel. If she is motor-sailing at night, then she would be lit as a power-driven vessel.

By day, the signals indicating the category of a privileged vessel may be hard to see. If a power-driven vessel is approaching a privileged vessel, and it appears not to have seen the signals, the privileged vessel can draw attention to herself by sounding the "wake-up" signal of at least five short and rapid blasts on the whistle (**Rule 34**). If the power-driven vessel still does not appear to be taking action to keep clear, then remember that under **Rule 17** (Action by Stand-on Vessel), the privileged vessel _may_ take action as soon as it becomes apparent that the give-way vessel is not taking action, and_must_ take action when a collision can no longer be avoided by the action of the give-way vessel alone.

> b. A sailing vessel underway shall keep out of the way of:
> i. a vessel not under command;
> ii. a vessel restricted in her ability to manoeuvre;
> iii. a vessel engaged in fishing.

For a sailing vessel to be considered as such, she must not be using a motor to help propel the vessel. If she is using a motor as well as sails to drive the vessel, then she is considered to be a power-driven vessel, and by day, she _must_ show a cone, apex down to signify that she is motor-sailing. If she is motor-sailing at night, then she must, of course, be lit as a power-driven vessel.

Not only must a sailing vessel keep out of the way of vessels not under command, restricted in their ability to manoeuvre and vessels fishing, but also, a sailing vessel must not impede the passage of a vessel which can only safely navigate within a narrow channel or fairway, (**Rule 9**), and must not impede the safe passage of a power-driven vessel which is following a traffic lane, (**Rule 10**). A sailing vessel is also obliged to keep clear of any vessel which she is overtaking, (**Rule 13**).

> c. A vessel engaged in fishing when underway shall, so far as possible, keep out of the way of:
> i. a vessel not under command;
> ii. a vessel restricted in her ability to manoeuvre.

A vessel is classed as a fishing vessel only when she is engaged in fishing, and using gear which restricts her ability to manoeuvre. On her way to, or from the fishing grounds, she is regarded as any other power-driven vessel.

When she is fishing, and displaying the appropriate signals, she is still obliged to keep watch, and to be prepared to manoeuvre for an approaching vessel which is not under command, or restricted in her ability to manoeuvre. She would also be expected to give way to another fishing vessel which was crossing on her starboard bow.

As well as keeping out of the way of vessels not under command, and vessels restricted in their ability to manoeuvre, fishing vessels are also required not to impede the passage of _any_ vessel navigating in a narrow channel or fairway (**Rule 9**), and are also required not to impede the passage of _any_ vessel following a traffic lane (**Rule 10**).

> d. i. Any vessel other than a vessel not under command or a vessel restricted in her ability to manoeuvre shall, if the circumstances of the case admit, avoid impeding the safe passage of a vessel constrained by her draught, exhibiting the signals in Rule 28.

Obviously a vessel not under command is probably unable to manoeuvre at all, and a vessel restricted in her ability to manoeuvre may have extreme difficulty in altering course, but all other vessels are expected to avoid impeding the safe passage of a vessel constrained by her draught.

Rule 3 defined a vessel as being constrained by her draught when she is limited in her ability to manoeuvre by the _width_ of the navigable channel which is available to her. **Rule 28** stipulates the signals that such a vessel must show – three red all-round lights in a vertical row by night, and a cylinder by day.

If a risk of collision develops, then both vessels must manoeuvre according to the Rules.

Remember that **Rule 1.b.** stated that local authorities are allowed to make special rules applicable in their waters. Often special rules are made to give extra privileges to vessels constrained by their draught. These rules might be to give special right-of-way to the constrained vessel, or to impose a moving exclusion zone around the vessel, forbidding any other vessel to approach within a given distance.

> ii. A vessel constrained by her draught shall navigate with particular caution having full regard to her special condition.

A vessel constrained by her draught can expect other vessels, except for those not under command, or restricted in their ability to manoeuvre, to avoid impeding her safe passage. However, there may be other circumstances when vessels which are required to keep out of the way do not do so, or perhaps cannot do so. Particularly by day, her signal denoting that she is constrained by her draught may not have been seen until the vessels are close. If such a situation occurs, and a risk of collision arises, then **Rule 8. iii.** told us that the vessel whose passage is not to be impeded, in this case, the vessel constrained by her draught, must navigate in accordance with the Rules if there is a risk of collision. So in this situation, for example, if the constrained vessel has a power-driven vessel crossing on her starboard bow, and that vessel has not taken **early and substantial action to keep well clear (Rule 16)**, and a risk of collision has developed, then the constrained vessel must navigate in accordance with the Rules to avoid a collision (**Rule 8.f.iii.**): she would sound one blast on the whistle, and initiate a turn to starboard, assuming that there were sufficient water.

Rule 17 (Action by Stand-on Vessel) says she <u>can</u> start to manoeuvre as soon as it becomes apparent that the other vessel is not taking appropriate action, and she <u>must</u> start to manoeuvre when collision cannot be avoided by the action of the give-way vessel alone. The first action that she would take would be to sound the wake-up signal – at least five short and rapid blasts on the whistle.

If a vessel constrained by her draught does begin to manoeuvre to avoid a collision, this action does not remove the responsibility of the other vessel to keep clear (**Rule 17.d.**).

Rule 6 told us that all vessels must proceed at a safe speed at all times. This includes vessels constrained by their draught, (**Rule 6.a.vi.** – vessels must take into account **the draught in relation to the available depth of water**). A vessel constrained by her draught should navigate at a speed which would enable her to stop in a reasonable distance if required, and be able to alter course if necessary to avoid a collision. Her engines must be kept ready to manoeuvre.

> c. A seaplane on the water shall, in general, keep well clear of all vessels and avoid impeding their navigation. In circumstances, however, where risk of collision exists, she shall comply with the Rules of this part.

Seaplanes, when on the water, must keep clear of all other vessels. If a situation arises where there is a risk of collision, then the seaplane, and indeed the other vessel, must manoeuvre in accordance with the Rules. This would include trying to avoid turns to port for vessels on her port side.

Hovercraft and hydrofoils are not considered as seaplanes, even when operating in a non-displacement mode. For the purposes of the Rules, they are treated as any other power-driven vessel. However, at night, in addition to the normal navigation lights, a hovercraft must show an all-round flashing yellow light (**Rule 23**). If there is much wind, a hovercraft may be pointed in a different direction from that in which she is travelling. It is often impossible to tell from the navigation lights in what direction she is travelling, so the flashing yellow light serves as a warning.

Although hovercraft, and high-speed hydrofoils are generally considered as normal power-driven vessels, because of their high speed, it would be considered good seamanship (**Rule 2**) for such craft to take early action to keep well clear of other, slower vessels.

When a vessel is required by this Rule to keep out of the way of another vessel, then **Rule 16** applies – the give-way vessel must **take early and substantial action to keep well clear**. This may be difficult in the case of one hampered vessel meeting another. If one is considered "less hampered" than the other, for example a fishing vessel meeting a vessel restricted in her ability to manoeuvre, then obviously the fishing vessel is obliged to keep clear. However, if two vessels classed in the same category meet, then both must manoeuvre so as to avoid a collision. They should both manoeuvre in accordance with the Rules, and that includes trying to avoid making turns to port to avoid vessels on their port side.

When a vessel is approaching a hampered vessel, **Rule 17** tells us that the stand-on vessel, in this case the hampered vessel, is supposed to hold her course and speed. However, this may not be possible in all cases, because of the nature of the work that the vessel is carrying out. Approaching vessels must be aware of this possibility.

Summary of Rule 18 – Responsibilities Between Vessels.

("Pecking Order" of vessels)

1. *Rule 18 applies to all vessels underway, that is all vessels not made fast to the shore, at anchor or aground. So it applies to vessels underway, but stopped in the water as well as to vessels making way through the water.*

2. *Except where Rule 9 (**N**ine for **N**arrow Channels), Rule 10 (**T**en for **T**raffic Separation) and Rule 13 (Overtaking) stipulate otherwise:*

A power-driven vessel keeps out of the way of a:
- *Vessel not under command;*
- *Vessel restricted in her ability to manoeuvre;*
- *Vessel fishing;*
- *Sailing vessel.*

A sailing vessel keeps out of the way of:
- *Vessel not under command;*
- *Vessel restricted in her ability to manoeuvre;*
- *Vessel fishing.*

A vessel fishing keeps out of the way of:
- *Vessel not under command;*
- *Vessel restricted in her ability to manoeuvre.*

3. *Everybody except vessels not under command and vessels restricted in their ability to manoeuvre must avoid impeding the safe passage of vessels constrained by their draught. Such vessels constrained by their draught must navigate at a safe speed with engines ready to manoeuvre.*

4. *Seaplanes on the water must keep clear of everybody, but if a risk of collision arises, they must navigate in accordance with the Rules.*

Part B.
STEERING AND SAILING RULES

SECTION THREE: Conduct of vessels in Restricted Visibility

Rule 19. Conduct of Vessels in Restricted Visibility

> a. This Rule applies to vessels not in sight of one another when navigating in or near an area of restricted visibility.

Rule 19 applies <u>only</u> when two vessels <u>cannot</u> see each other. If vessels detect each other by radar, but cannot see each other by eye, then **Rule 19** applies. However, if they subsequently get close enough for one to be able to see the other, then **Rule 19** no longer applies, and the "normal" Rules of **Section II**, Conduct of Vessels in Sight of One Another (**Rules 11 to 18**) apply.

Rule 19 cannot be taken to apply when a vessel did not see another just because a bad look-out was being kept. If it is possible to see one vessel from the other, then the Rules of **Section II** apply.

The term **restricted visibility** was defined in **Rule 3** as **any condition in which visibility is restricted by fog, mist, falling snow, heavy rainstorms, sandstorms or any other similar causes.**

Notice that **Rule 19** is applicable not only when vessels are in restricted visibility, but also when navigating **near** such areas. A vessel passing close offshore of a coastal fog bank must comply with **Rule 19**, and must also sound the appropriate fog signals as stipulated in **Rule 35**, even though the vessel is itself in good visibility. These fog signals are the only sound signals which should be sounded in restricted visibility. When two vessels are manoeuvring, but are not in sight of each other, they should not sound the manoeuvring signals that are stipulated in **Rule 34**.

> b. Every vessel shall proceed at a safe speed adapted to the prevailing circumstances and conditions of restricted visibility. A power-driven vessel shall have her engines ready for immediate manoeuvre.

Rule 6 told us that vessels must **at all times proceed at a safe speed**, and it specifically mentions the visibility as one of the factors to consider when determining what is a

safe speed. Other factors listed in **Rule 6** include the manoeuvrability of the vessel, availability and efficiency of radar, the presence of other vessels, and the possibility of small vessels, or ice, which may not show on the radar.

A vessel on the high seas, several hundred miles from land, that has an efficient radar, would probably be justified in navigating at a higher speed than it would be when passing through dense shipping, or when navigating in an area where small vessels or ice could be encountered. Any power-driven vessel must have her engines ready to manoeuvre if visibility is reduced, even if a relatively high speed is justified by the circumstances.

> c. Every vessel shall have due regard to the prevailing circumstances and conditions of restricted visibility when complying with the Rules of Section I of this Part, (i.e. Part B, The Steering and Sailing Rules).

Section I of **Part B** covers **Rules 4 to 10** – the Rules that apply in all conditions of visibility. The Rules with particular relevance are:

Rule 5 – Look-out. This tells us to **maintain a proper look-out by sight and by hearing as well as by all available means appropriate to the prevailing circumstances and conditions**. In dense fog, an aural look-out is at least as, but possibly even more, important than a visual look-out. The term **all available means** is taken to include radar, if fitted, and in many cases a listening watch on the VHF radio for warnings of movements of other vessels, as well as an aural and visual look-out.

Rule 6 – Safe Speed. A vessel must **at all times proceed at a safe speed so that she can take proper and effective action to avoid collision and be stopped within a distance appropriate to the prevailing circumstances and conditions**. A speed which allows a vessel to stop within half the distance of visibility is often held to be a safe speed. Some circumstances and conditions may dictate a slower speed. **Rule 6** specifically mentions visibility as one of the factors to consider in determining a safe speed, both in **Section a.** which concerns all vessels, and in **Section b**. which is applicable to vessels fitted with radar.

Rule 7 – Risk of Collision. This Rule states that **all available means** must be used to determine if a risk of collision exists. It then specifically mentions radar, and that if radar is available, then **radar plotting or the equivalent** must be used to assess the risk of collision. It also says that if there is any doubt, then a risk of collision must be assumed to exist.

Rule 8 – Action to Avoid a Collision. **Rule 8** states that any action taken to avoid a collision must be **positive**, and **made in ample time**. It also says that any action must be **large enough to be readily apparent** to the other vessel, and if more time is needed to assess a situation, then the vessel should be slowed or stopped.

Rule 9 – Narrow Channels, and **Rule 10** – Traffic Separation Schemes, apply at all times, so their effect must be taken into consideration in restricted visibility, particularly by small vessels, or sailing vessels intending to cross a narrow channel or traffic lane. They must do so without impeding other vessels in the narrow channel or traffic lane.

> d. A vessel which detects by radar alone the presence of another vessel shall determine if a close-quarters situation is developing and/or risk of collision exists. If so, she shall take avoiding action in ample time, provided that when such action consists of an alteration of course, so far as possible the following shall be avoided:
>
> i. an alteration of course to port for a vessel forward of the beam, other than for a vessel being overtaken;
> iii. an alteration of course towards a vessel abeam or abaft the beam.

For a vessel to detect another vessel **by radar alone**, it means that the other vessel has not been sighted, <u>nor has its fog signal been heard</u>.

If the vessel has been sighted, then **Rule 19** ceases to apply. Instead the Rules of **Section II** – Conduct of Vessels in Sight of One Another, i.e. **Rules 11 to 18**, come into effect.

We shall see that in **Rule 19.e.**, if a fog signal is heard forward of the beam, then the vessel must **reduce her speed to a minimum at which she can be kept on course**. Obviously a good watch must be kept by sight and by hearing if this part of the Rule is to be observed.

None of the Rules in **Section II** – Conduct of Vessels in Sight of One Another, Rules 11 to 18, refer to a **close-quarters situation**, they only refer to **risk of collision**.

When two vessels cannot see each other, **Rule 19** is directing us not only to avoid a risk of collision, but to avoid a close-quarters situation as well.

A close-quarters situation is hard to quantify, and it depends on a number of factors, including the visibility, manoeuvrability of the vessels, density of other shipping, proximity to navigational hazards, and depth of water available. In open sea, a close-quarters situation would probably be considered as about two miles, which is the required audible range of the whistle of a large vessel. In confined waters, when navigating at slow speed, in dense traffic, much shorter distances would have to be accepted.

If the vessels are in restricted waters, such as a narrow channel, and a close-quarters situation is developing, but there is <u>no risk</u> of collision, then there is no need to take action. However, in open waters, action must be taken **in ample time**, to avoid a close-quarters situation. This applies regardless of the direction from which the other vessel approaches. When **Rule 19** applies, there are no stand-on vessels. Not even a vessel being overtaken is allowed to maintain her course, if she detects by radar the approach of an overtaking vessel, which will result in a close-quarters situation. This is because the vessel being overtaken does not know if the other vessel has radar, or has detected her on their radar. So each and every vessel is obliged to take avoiding action, without relying on the actions of others.

Section **d.i.** says that for vessels forward of the beam alterations to port are to be avoided, as far as possible, except when overtaking. This is to encourage a "port-to-port" passing situation, because, if the vessels get close enough to see each other, then **Rule 19** ceases to apply, **and Rules 14** – Head-on Situation, **15** – Crossing Situation, and **17** – Action by Stand-on Vessel, apply. These Rules effectively place a similar restriction on vessels altering to port, if there is a risk of collision. A vessel turning to port to avoid a crossing vessel could substantially increase the risk of collision, if the other vessel is acting in accordance with the Rules, and is altering to starboard.

An alteration to port is permissible when overtaking, both under **Rule 19**, and under the "visual" Rules. Bear in mind though, that if a vessel in restricted visibility, detects by radar an overtaking vessel approaching on her starboard quarter, she should be initiating an alteration of course away from the overtaking vessel, which in this case will be an alteration to port.

Section **d.ii.** says that we must try not to alter course towards a vessel abeam, or abaft the beam. This means that if a vessel is approaching in the quadrant from the starboard beam to the stern, then the correct action for the vessel being overtaken would be a turn to port, away from the approaching vessel. For vessels approaching in any of the other three quadrants, i.e. for any vessel approaching on the port quarter, port bow, or the starboard bow, then alterations to port should be avoided, so far as possible.

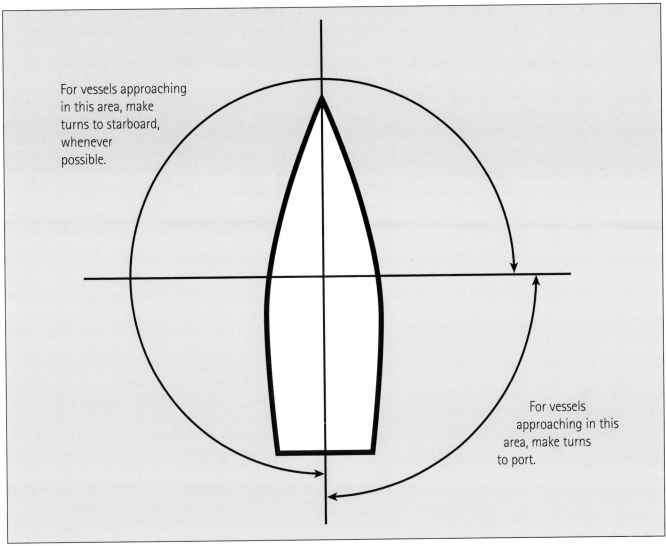

For vessels approaching in this area, make turns to starboard, whenever possible.

For vessels approaching in this area, make turns to port.

Figure 19.1 For vessels approaching from the port quarter, port bow or the starboard bow, make turns to starboard, whenever possible. For vessels approaching from the starboard quarter, turns to port are not only permissible, but are advisable.

The Rule does allow for exceptions, by saying **so far as possible**. Because of the proximity of other vessels, or perhaps because of a lack of navigable water to starboard, an alteration to port may be the only option. If this be the case, then the alteration must be done soon enough, and it must be done boldly enough to be readily apparent to the other vessel. If it is in restricted waters, then it may be possible to advise the other vessel of your intentions by VHF, perhaps identifying yourself by giving your position in relation to a navigational mark.

> e.   Except where it has been determined that a risk of collision does not exist, every vessel which hears apparently forward of her beam the fog signal of another vessel, or which cannot avoid a close-quarters situation with another vessel forward of her beam, shall reduce her speed to the minimum at which she can be kept on her course. She shall if necessary take all her way off and in any event navigate with extreme caution until danger of collision is over.

If a fog signal is heard, then **paragraph d.** cannot apply, because the vessel has not been detected by radar alone.

If the vessels are close enough for the fog signals to be heard, then it can be taken that a close-quarters situation exists. The intensity of the sound signals for vessels of various sizes is given in **Annex III**. The expected audible range, in still air for signals from each class of vessel is:

- Vessels over 200 metres in length   2 miles
- 75 to 200 metres in length   1.5 miles
- 20 to 75 metres in length   1 mile
- less than 20 metres in length   0.5 miles.

If a fog signal is heard forward of the beam, then the vessel <u>must</u> **reduce speed to the minimum at which she can be kept on her course**, unless it has been determined that a risk of collision does not exist. Such a case might occur when two vessels are navigating in opposite directions in a narrow channel. Another vessel has been plotted by radar on a closing course, but it has been determined that the vessels will pass clear. If they then pass close enough for the fog signal to be heard, it could be deemed safe to proceed, but great care must be taken to ensure that the fog signal is coming from the vessel which is being plotted, and not from another, which has not yet been detected by the radar.

Rule 7 – Risk of Collision, told us that **Assumptions shall not be made on the basis of scanty information, especially scanty radar information**. A vessel must not alter course when another vessel is detected, either by radar or by hearing a fog signal, until the course of that vessel is known. If the vessel is detected by radar, then it must be plotted (**Rule 7.b.**), and its course determined. If it is only detected by the sound of the fog signal, and it is forward of the beam, then **19.e.** is telling us we must slow down or stop, until the danger of collision is over.

If the course of the other vessel has been determined, and it is decided that an alteration of course is necessary, then remember that the first paragraph of this Rule tells us to try to avoid altering to port for any vessel forward of the beam.

If a vessel hears the fog signal from another vessel indicating it is stopped in the water, (two prolonged blasts), then it must not be assumed that the vessel will remain stopped. It could start moving at any moment, so extreme care must be taken, until the danger has passed.

Particular care must also be taken if the signal heard indicates a hampered vessel. One prolonged and two short blasts could indicate a vessel which is:

- Not under command;
- Restricted in ability to manoeuvre;
- Fishing;
- Under sail;
- Towing another vessel.

If such a signal is heard, then particular attention should be paid to listening for the possibility of a fog signal from a towed vessel – one prolonged and three short blasts. It is no use navigating safely astern of an approaching tug, only to cross in front of its tow.

A lookout placed forward will often be able to hear fog signals which cannot be heard from the bridge of a large vessel or the cockpit of a smaller one. Such a lookout should be posted whenever the visibility is much reduced. This is not only good seamanship, it is required by **Rule 4** – Lookout.

Summary of Rule 19 – Conduct of vessels in Restricted Visibility.

1. *Rule 19 applies to all vessels operating in or <u>near</u> an area of poor visibility, and only applies when the vessels cannot see each other. As soon as they sight one another, then the "normal" steering Rules apply. When Rule 19 applies, the only sound signals which should be given are the appropriate fog signals.*

2. *Under Rule 19, there are no "stand-on" vessels. <u>Any vessel which detects another vessel <u>by radar alone</u> must determine if there is a risk of collision, or of a <u>close-quarters situation</u> arising. If there is such a risk, then avoiding action must be taken. Such action must be taken in <u>ample time</u>, and if the action is an alteration of course, then so far as possible, <u>alterations to port should be avoided</u> for vessels forward of the beam except when overtaking. For vessels abeam or abaft the beam, <u>alterations towards the other vessel should be avoided, so far as possible</u>.*

3. *If a fog signal is heard forward of the beam, unless it has been determined that there is no risk of collision, then the vessel must slow down or stop, until the danger has passed.*

Part C.
LIGHTS AND SHAPES
Rules 20 - 31

Rule 20. Application

> a. Rules in this Part shall be complied with in all weathers.

All vessels, even small vessels, are required to show the appropriate lights and shapes required by the Rules. If a light or shape is lost, perhaps because of heavy weather, it must be replaced or repaired as soon as possible.

> b. The Rules concerning lights shall be complied with from sunset to sunrise, and during such times no other lights shall be exhibited, except such lights as cannot be mistaken for the lights specified in these Rules or do not impair their visibility or distinctive character, or interfere with the keeping of a proper look-out.

The correct lights shall be shown from sunset to sunrise, and during this period, no other lights which can cause confusion may be shown. Lights which make it difficult to see the specified lights, or which interfere with keeping a look-out must not be shown. All too often, fishing vessels are a blaze of working lights which ignore all of the above!

When we get to **Rule 30** – Anchored Vessels and Vessels Aground – we shall see that vessels over 100 metres in length must, and smaller vessels may, use their decklights when at anchor, to make the vessel more conspicuous. Such lights should be turned off when the anchor light(s) are turned off, as soon as the anchor has broken out. At the same time, the navigation lights should be turned on, since the moment that the anchor has broken out, the vessel is deemed to be underway.

> c. The lights prescribed by these Rules shall, if carried, also be exhibited from sunrise to sunset in restricted visibility and may be exhibited in all other circumstances when it is deemed necessary.

If a vessel is fitted with navigation lights, then she must show them by day, in restricted visibility, and she may also show them under other circumstances if it is felt necessary.

> d. The Rules concerning shapes shall be complied with by day.

The term "by day" suggests that the shapes should be carried during twilight, as well as from sunrise to sunset. Since lights must be shown from sunset to sunrise, during twilight periods both lights and shapes should be shown. Twilight can be thought of as the period after the sun has set, or before it has risen, when there is sufficient light to see another vessel.

> e. The lights and shapes specified in these Rules shall comply with the provisions of Annex I to these regulations.

Annex I gives all the specifications for the lights and shapes which are required by **Part C** of the Rules.

Summary of Rule 20 – Application of the Rules for Lights and Shapes.

1. *The correct lights and shapes must be carried in all weathers.*
2. *The correct lights must be shown from sunset to sunrise, and when in restricted visibility, and whenever else they could be useful.*
3. *Day signals must be carried by day, so both lights and shapes should be carried during twilight periods.*
4. *Lights and shapes are specified in Annex I of the Rules.*
5. *Any other lights which are carried must be such that they cannot be confused with lights specified in the Rules, they must not prevent the stipulated lights from being seen, nor may they interfere with the ability of the lookout to see.*

Rule 21. Definitions

This Rule gives the general definitions of colour, position on the vessel, and arcs of visibility for each type of light which is specified in **Part C** of the Rules. This allows an understanding of which lights will be visible, from different bearings, for various types of vessel. Detailed specifications of the lights are given in **Annex I** of these Rules. We will refer to the most important parts of **Annex I** as we go through the Rules.

> a. "Masthead light" means a white light placed over the fore and aft centreline of the vessel showing an unbroken light over an arc of the horizon of 225 degrees and so fixed as to show the light from right ahead to 22.5 degrees abaft the beam on either side of the vessel.

Nowhere in the Rules does it state that a "masthead light" must be placed on a mast! **Annex 1, Section 2.f.i.** states that it must **be so placed as to be above and clear of all other lights and obstructions**. A masthead light shows through the arc from 22.5° abaft the beam, through the bows, to 22.5° abaft the other beam. It is, by definition, white. The coloured lights such as those specified for

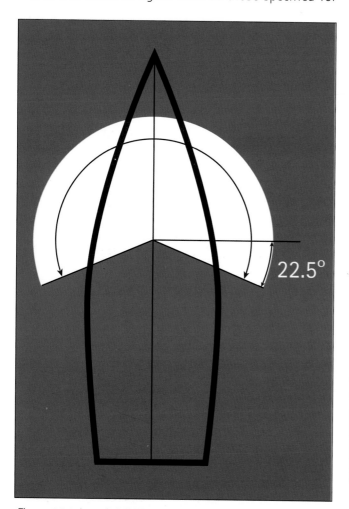

Figure 21.1 Arc of visibility of a masthead light.

vessels not under command, restricted in ability to manoeuvre, fishing vessels and sailing vessels are all-round lights.

> b. "Sidelights" means a green light on the starboard side and a red light on the port side, each showing an unbroken light over an arc of the horizon of 112.5 degrees and so fixed as to show the light from right ahead to 22.5 degrees abaft the beam on its respective side. In a vessel of less than 20 metres in length the sidelights may be combined in one lantern carried on the fore and aft centreline of the vessel.

Sidelights are red on the port side and green on the starboard. They must show over an unbroken arc from ahead to 22.5° abaft the beam. Vessels under 20 metres may combine the two lights as a single lantern.

Annex 1, Section 5 states that vessels over 20 metres in length <u>must</u> be fitted with matt black screens inboard of the lights, to screen the correct arcs of visibility. Smaller vessels may be fitted with such screens if needed, to make the lights comply with the acs of visibility. If the lights are combined as a single lantern, on a vessel of less than 20 metres, then there must be a "very narrow" division between the red and green sectors.

Annex 1, Section 9 stipulates that the cut-off of the sidelights in the forward direction must be at 1° to 3° beyond the prescribed sectors. This slight overlap of the sidelights in the forward direction ensures that another vessel approaching end-on will see the sidelights, and there is no possibility of a dark sector between the lights.

> c. "Sternlight" means a white light placed as nearly as practicable at the stern showing an unbroken light over an arc of the horizon of 135 degrees and so fixed as to show the light 67.5 degrees from right aft on each side of the vessel.

The sternlight is a white light which shows through the arc that the sidelights and masthead lights do not, i.e. from 22.5° abaft the beam, through the stern, to 22.5° abaft the other beam.

If another vessel can see the stern light, then it is 22.5° or more abaft the beam, so it is an overtaking vessel – **Rule 13**.

The words "placed as nearly as practicable at the stern" are there to accommodate those vessels which find it difficult or impossible to place the light at the stern.

> d. "Towing light" means a yellow light having the same characteristics as the "sternlight" defined in paragraph c. of this Rule.

The towing light is shown by vessels towing another vessel astern, and it is shown vertically above the sternlight.

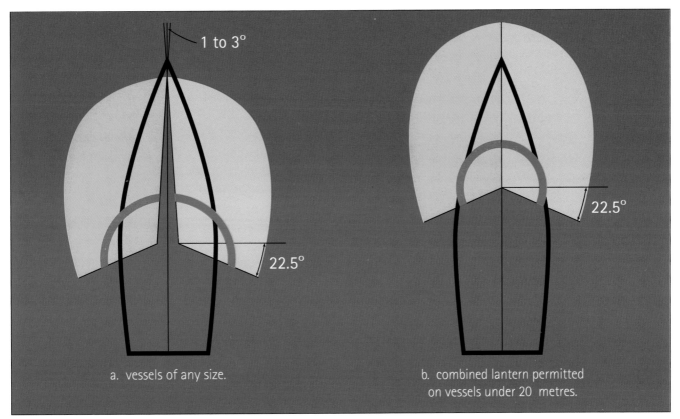

a. vessels of any size.

b. combined lantern permitted on vessels under 20 metres.

Figure 21.2 Arcs of visibility of sidelights:

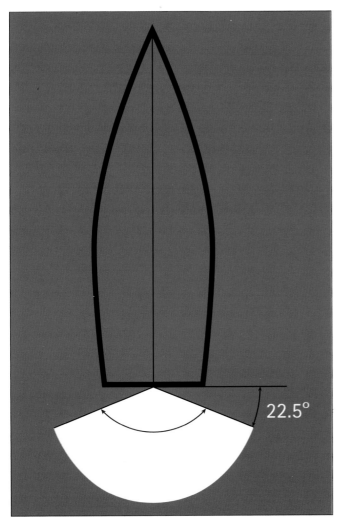

Figure 21.3 Arc of visibility of the stern light

It shows through the same arc as the sternlight. A tug which is pushing ahead, or towing alongside, does not normally exhibit the towing light, (**Rule 24** – Towing and pushing) although in some coastal states, local rules stipulate that they shall.

> e. "All-round" light means a light showing an unbroken light over an arc of the horizon of 360 degrees.

Annex 1, Section 9, accepts that it may not be practical to have an unbroken arc of visibility, but it stipulates that no dark sector may be more than 6°. If this is impossible to achieve with a single light, then two lights may be placed close to each other, and suitably screened, so as to appear as a single light.

> f. "Flashing light" means a light flashing at regular intervals at a frequency of 120 flashes or more per minute.

A flashing yellow light must be shown by air-cushion vessels (such as hovercraft), when operating in the non-displacement mode. Submarines may show a flashing amber light when on the surface. The high rate of flashing of 120 flashes per minute differentiates such lights from flashing navigational aids, which rarely flash at more than half that rate.

An exception to this Rule is the pair of flashing yellow lights which are shown by purse seine fishing vessels. The two lights flash alternately every second, with equal periods of light and dark (isophase).

Local Rules may specify additional lights. For example many Coastal States specify flashing blue lights to be shown by some government vessels, such as police or fire vessels.

Summary of Rule 21 – Definitions of Lights.

1. *Masthead lights show from 22.5° abaft the beam, through the bows, to 22.5° abaft the other beam. By definition, a masthead light is white.*
2. *Sidelights show from 22.5° abaft the beam to ahead, with the cut-off point 1 to 3° on the opposite bow. The overlap ensures that there is no dark sector ahead.*
3. *Sternlights and towing lights show from 22.5° abaft the beam, through the stern, to 22.5° abaft the other beam.*
4. *All-round lights can have dark sectors up to 6°. An all-round light can be replaced with two lights, close to each other, and suitably screened so as to appear as one light.*
5. *A flashing light, when stipulated by this section of the Rules, (hovercraft and sometimes submarines), must flash at 120 flashes per second or more, so as not to be confused with flashing navigational aids.*

Rule 22. Visibility of Lights

The lights prescribed in these Rules shall have an intensity as specified in Section 8 of Annex I to these Regulations so as to be visible at the following minimum ranges:

a. In vessels of 50 metres or more in length:
- a masthead light, 6 miles;
- a sidelight, 3 miles;
- a sternlight, 3 miles;
- a towing light, 3 miles;
- a white, red, green or yellow all-round light, 3 miles.

b. In vessels of 12 metres or more in length but less than 50 metres in length:
- a masthead light, 5 miles, except that where the length of the vessel is less than 20 metres, 3 miles;
- a sidelight, 2 miles;
- a sternlight, 2 miles;
- a towing light, 2 miles;
- a white, red, green or yellow all-round light, 2 miles.

c. In vessels of less than 12 metres in length:
- a masthead light, 2 miles;

- a sidelight, 1 mile;
- a sternlight, 2 miles;
- a towing light, 2 miles;
- a white, red, green or yellow all-round light, 2 miles.

d. In inconspicuous, partly submerged vessels or objects being towed:
- a white all-round light, 3 miles.

Section 8 of Annex 1 gives a formula for calculating how bright a light must be, to be "visible" from a given distance, under particular conditions. This "brightness", or luminous intensity, is given in candelas.

Most light bulbs for navigation lights are marked with their wattage. If a bulb is to be replaced, then one of the same power should be selected to ensure that the navigation light meets the requirements. Bulbs for lights which shine through a specified arc will normally have a vertical filament. This helps to give a sharp cut-off point to the arc of visibility.

Section 8 also warns that the maximum luminous intensity of navigation lights should be limited, to avoid undue glare. It then states that a variable control, or dimmer switch should not be used to reduce the brightness. It would be too easy for the switch to be set too low, and for the lights to fail to meet the brightness requirements.

The white, red, green or yellow all-round lights are those used for indications such as: not under command, restricted in ability to manoeuvre etc., and also include the anchor lights.

Summary of Rule 22 – Visibility of lights.

The list of the visible range of lights looks rather daunting to learn, but in fact, once it is broken down, it is not too bad. The first thing to remember is that masthead lights, being higher than the others, are the first ones that an approaching ship can see, so they need to be the brightest. Also, white lights, for the same power, have a greater range of visibility than coloured lights. Let's look at the stipulated ranges:

- *Vessels over 50 metres – 6 miles for the masthead lights, 3 miles for all the rest.*
- *Vessels 20 to 50 metres – 5 miles for the masthead lights, 2 miles for all the rest.*
- *Vessels 12 to 20 metres – 3 miles for the masthead lights, 2 miles for all the rest.*
- *Vessels under 12 metres – 2 miles for everything, except 1 mile for the coloured sidelights.*
- *Inconspicuous objects being towed – 3 mile all-round white.*

The luminous intensity of the various lights is specified in Annex1.

Rule 23. Power-driven Vessels Underway

a. A power-driven vessel underway shall exhibit:
i. a masthead light forward;
ii. a second masthead light abaft of and higher than the forward one; except that a vessel of less than 50 metres in length shall not be obliged to exhibit such light, but may do so;
iii. sidelights;
iv. a sternlight.

Annex 1, sections 2 and 3, contain stipulations about the positioning of the various lights. The arcs of visibility for each light were stipulated in **Rule 21** – Definitions.

Remember that **Rule 21** told us that any vessel less than 20 metres in length can combine the sidelights in a single lantern.

Between sunset and sunrise, or in restricted visibility, a power-driven vessel must show all the lights <u>whenever it is underway</u>, i.e. it is not aground, not anchored nor made fast to the shore. It does not have to be making way through the water.

However, we will see in **Rule 26** that fishing vessels show their sidelights and stern lights <u>only when making way</u> through the water, and that **Rule 27** stipulates that vessels not under command show their sidelights and stern lights <u>only when making way</u>, and vessels restricted in their ability to manoeuvre show sidelights stern lights and masthead lights <u>only when making way</u> through the water.

b. An air-cushion vessel when operating in the non-displacement mode, shall, in addition to the lights prescribed in paragraph a. of this Rule, exhibit an all-round flashing yellow light.

The original purpose of the flashing yellow light was to warn others that the hovercraft was operating in the non-displacement mode. When such a vessel is operating, it is very susceptible to the wind, and it can often be travelling in a direction rather different to that indicated by the navigation lights. Local Rules may allow hydrofoils and other high speed vessels, which are not air-cushion type vessels, to show the flashing yellow light. Such vessels will be travelling in the direction indicated by their navigation lights, but at higher speeds than conventional vessels.

Submarines on the surface may show a flashing amber light – this can easily be mistaken for a yellow light. If it is shown, it is carried above the after (higher) masthead light.

c.i. A power-driven vessel of less than 12 metres in length may in lieu of the lights prescribed in paragraph a. of this Rule, exhibit an all-round white light and side lights;

A small power-driven vessel less than 12 metres is allowed to have a single all-round white light, instead of the masthead light and stern light. It must still show the sidelights, unless it is less than 7 metres, and is not capable of more than 7 knots, when, as we shall see in the next paragraph, it is allowed to show a single all-round white light.

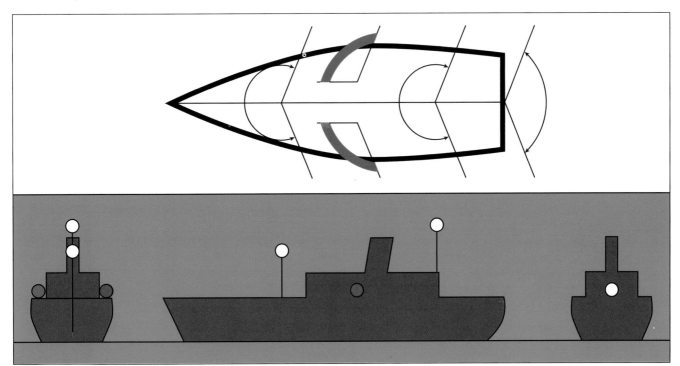

Figure 23.1 Lights for power-driven vessels underway:
a. Vessels over 50 metres, or, optionally for vessels under 50 metres in length.

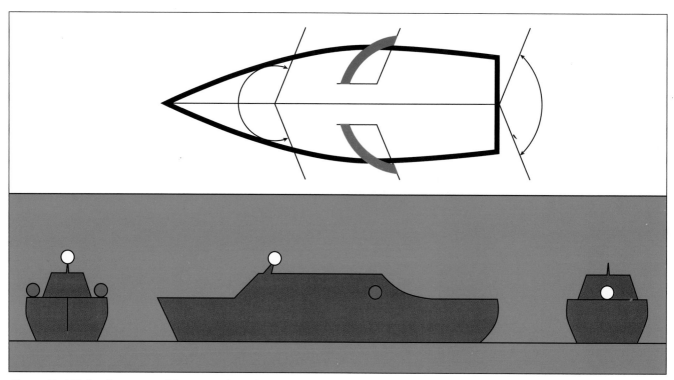

Figure 23.1 Lights for power-driven vessels underway:
  b. Vessels under 50 metres in length.

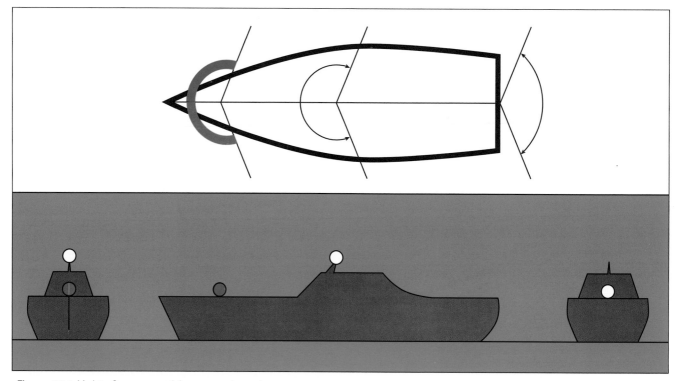

Figure 23.1 Lights for power-driven vessels underway:
  c. Optional lights for vessels under 20 metres in length.

ii. a power-driven vessel of less than 7 metres in length whose maximum speed does not exceed 7 knots may in lieu of the lights prescribed in paragraph a. of this Rule exhibit an all-round white light and shall, if practicable, also exhibit sidelights;

A power-driven vessel of less than 7 metres, if its designed maximum speed is less than 7 knots, may show a single all-round white light, instead of the normal navigation lights. Such a light must be shown at all times at night in a power-driven vessel. We shall see in **Rule 25**, that a sailing vessel under 7 metres does not have to show a light continuously, but is allowed to show a light "in sufficient time to prevent a collision".

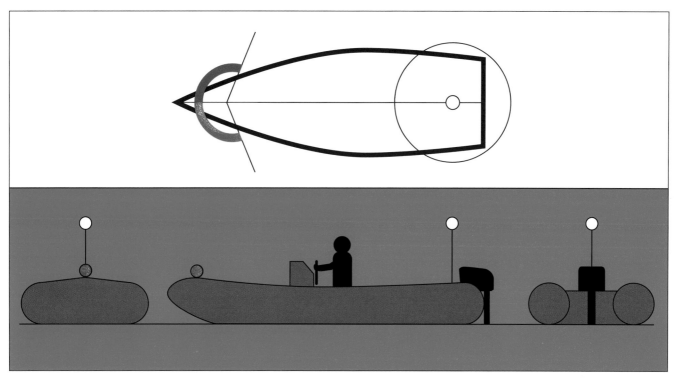

Figure 23.2 Lights for a power-driven vessel less than 12 metres in length.

This exemption does not apply to craft <u>capable</u> of more than 7 knots, even if they are navigating slowly. If the vessel is <u>capable</u> of more than 7 knots, it must show the sidelights, as well as an all-round white, or masthead light and stern light, even if it is going at a slow speed.

All vessels should show sidelights if practicable.

> iii. the masthead light or all-round white light on a power-driven vessel of less than 12 metres in length may be displaced from the fore and aft centreline of the vessel if centreline fitting is not practicable, provided that the sidelights are combined in one lantern which shall be carried on the fore and aft centreline of the vessel or located as nearly as practicable in the same fore and aft line as the masthead light or the all-round white light.

The masthead or all-round white light may be offset from the centre-line if necessary, but if it is, then the sidelights must be combined in a single lantern, which should be on the centreline, or on the same fore and aft line as the white light. This is to try and retain the correct aspect of the lights, when seen from another vessel.

It may be difficult to mount the all-round white light on the centreline of an open launch with an offset steering console, or one powered by a large outboard engine. This section of the Rule allows the light to mounted in a more convenient location.

In some places, local Rules allow for the masthead light and stern light to be replaced by an all-round white light on vessels larger than 12 metres.

Summary of Rule 23 – Power-driven Vessels.

1. *A power-driven vessel must show all the stipulated lights whenever it is underway i.e. not aground, not at anchor nor made fast to the shore. It does not have to be making way through the water. (Fishing vessels, vessels not under command and vessels restricted in their ability to manoeuvre show their sidelights and stern lights only when making way through the water.)*

2. *Power-driven vessels over 50 metres <u>must</u> and other vessels <u>may</u> show a second masthead light above and abaft of the masthead light.*

3. *Power-driven vessels less than 20 metres in length may combine the sidelights in a single lantern, and those less than 12 metres in length may combine the masthead and stern light in a single all-round white light.*

4. *Power-driven vessels less than 7 metres, and <u>capable</u> of less than 7 knots, may show a single all-round white, instead of the other lights.*

5. *Air-cushion vessels operating in the non-displacement mode must show an all-round flashing yellow light, in addition to the required navigation lights.*

Rule 24. Towing and Pushing

> a. A power-driven vessel when towing shall exhibit:
> i. instead of the light prescribed in Rule 23 a. i. (forward masthead light) or a. ii. (after masthead light), two masthead lights in a vertical line. When

> the length of the tow, measuring from the stern of the towing vessel to the after end of the tow, exceeds 200 metres, three such lights in a vertical line;
> ii. sidelights;
> iii. a stern light;
> iv. a towing light in a vertical line above the stern light;
> v. when the length of the tow exceeds 200 metres, a diamond shape where it can best be seen.

The length of a tow is measured from the stern of the tug to the stern of the towed vessel or object.

The additional two or three white lights which indicate a tug, are classed as masthead lights, so they show through the same arc as any other masthead light – from 22.5° abaft the beam, through the bows, to 22.5° abaft the other beam. They are not all-round lights. From astern, only the normal stern light, and the yellow towing light positioned above it, and showing through the same arc, will be visible. The yellow towing light is only specified for vessels towing another vessel or object astern. We will see that for vessels towing alongside, or pushing ahead, there is no yellow towing light specified in the International Rules, but some coastal states have a local rule, stipulating that the yellow towing light must be shown under these circumstances.

The additional two, or three, masthead lights of a tug can replace either the forward, or the after (higher) masthead light of a normal power-driven vessel.

Annex 1, Section 2 specifies the positioning of the masthead lights. If the lights replace the after masthead light, then the lowest of them must be 4.5 metres above the forward masthead light. The additional masthead lights must be at least 2 metres apart on a vessel over 20 metres,

and at least 1 metre apart on a vessel under 20 metres.

By day, if the length of the tow (from the stern of the tug to the stern of the towed vessel) does not exceed 200 metres, then there is no day signal to be shown by the towing vessel. If the length of the tow is more than 200 metres, then the towing vessel must show a diamond shape, where it can best be seen. **Annex 1, Section 6** defines the diamond shape. It must be black, and be formed by two cones suspended base-to-base. The diameter of the base, and the height of each cone must be at least 0.6 metre.

The towed vessel must show a similar diamond when the length of the tow is more than 200 metres.

> b. When a pushing vessel and a vessel being pushed ahead are rigidly connected in a composite unit they shall be regarded as a power-driven vessel and exhibit the lights prescribed in Rule 23.

When a tug is pushing ahead, and the two vessels are rigidly connected, so as to effectively form a single vessel, the unit is lit as a single power-driven vessel. **Rule 23** specifies the lights for a power-driven vessel, i.e. masthead lights, sidelights and stern light. No extra lights or signals are shown.

> c. A power-driven vessel when pushing ahead or towing alongside, except in the case of a composite unit, shall exhibit:
> i. instead of the light prescribed in Rule 23 a. i. or a. ii. (The forward or after masthead light of a power-driven vessel.) Two masthead lights in a vertical line;
> ii. sidelights;
> iii. a sternlight.

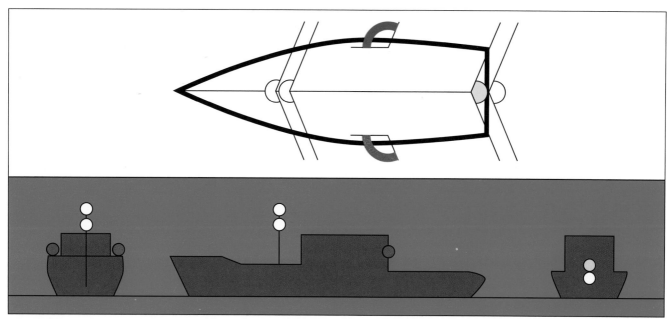

Figure 24.1
  a. Tug less than 50 metres in length, with a tow 200 metres or less, in length.

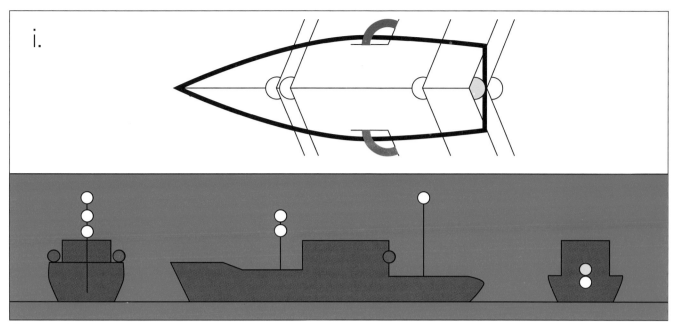

Figure 24.1
   b. *Tug over 50 metres (or possibly less) in length, with a tow 200 metres or less, in length – i. or ii.*

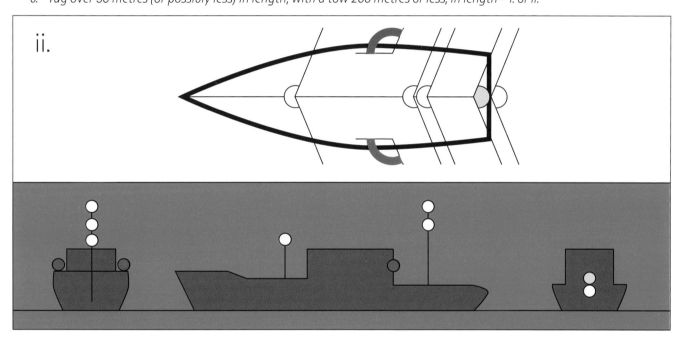

A tug pushing ahead, or towing alongside, shows the same pair of masthead lights as a tug with a tow astern, of less than 200 metres. The lights are shown one above the other, in lieu of either the normal forward or after masthead light. Note that there is no yellow towing light specified – such a light is only for vessels towing astern, although this Rule is often modified by coastal states, who may stipulate that the yellow towing light is also shown when pushing ahead and/or when towing alongside.

A vessel being pushed ahead must show side lights, and a vessel being towed alongside must show sidelights and a stern light.

If a tug which is towing astern, pushing ahead or towing alongside is over 50 metres long, it <u>must</u> show the second masthead light of a power-driven vessel over 50 metres. It <u>may</u> show such a light if it is under 50 metres long.

Remember that the two or three additional masthead lights in a vertical line, indicating a tug, can replace either the forward or the after masthead light of a power-driven vessel.

> d.   A power-driven vessel to which Paragraphs a. or c. of this Rule apply shall also comply with Rule 23 a. ii.

> e.   A vessel or object being towed, other than those mentioned in Paragraph g. of this Rule, shall exhibit:
> i.   sidelights;
> ii. a stern light;
> iii. when the length of the tow exceeds 200 metres, a diamond shape where it can best be seen.

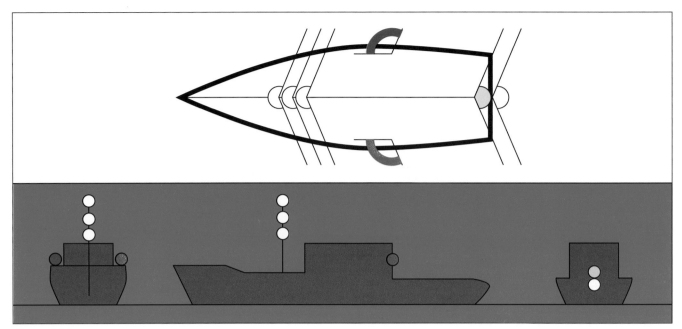

Figure 24.1

   c. Tug less than 50 metres in length, with a tow more than 200 metres in length.

Paragraph g. refers to inconspicuous or partly submerged vessels or objects being towed, and they have their own specific lights.

This section refers only to vessels or objects being towed astern. The next section covers those being towed alongside or pushed ahead.

Vessels being towed astern must show side lights and a stern light.

By day, if the length of the tow, from the stern of the tug to the stern of the tow, does not exceed 200 metres, then there is no day signal to be shown, unless the tow is a partly submerged or inconspicuous object, when the day signal is shown regardless of the length. If the length of the tow does exceed 200 metres, then the towed vessel must show a diamond shape, as was specified for the towing vessel.

> f.   Provided that any number of vessels being towed alongside or pushed in a group shall be lighted as one vessel:
> i.   a vessel being pushed ahead, not being part of a composite unit, shall exhibit at the forward end, sidelights;
> ii. a vessel being towed alongside shall exhibit a sternlight and at the forward end, sidelights.

If a group of vessels are being pushed ahead as a unit, or towed alongside, they must be lit as a single unit.

Vessels towed alongside must show sidelights and a stern light, while those being pushed ahead do not need to show a stern light.

> g.   An inconspicuous, partly submerged vessel or object, or combination of such vessels or objects being towed, shall exhibit:

> i.   if it is less than 25 metres in breadth, one all-round white light at or near the forward end and one at or near the after end except that dracones (flexible floating tank, usually used for carrying oil) need not exhibit a light at or near the forward end;
> ii. if it is 25 metres or more in breadth, two additional all-round white lights at or near the extremities of its breadth;
> iii. if it exceeds 100 metres in length, additional all-round white lights between the lights prescribed in subparagraphs i. and ii. So that the distance between the lights shall not exceed 100 metres;
> iv. a diamond shape at or near the aftermost extremity of the last vessel or object being towed and if the length of the tow exceeds 200 metres an additional diamond shape where it can best be seen and located as far forward as is practicable.

An inconspicuous or partly submerged vessel or object must be lit as follows:

- An all-round white light at each end. (Except that dracones – flexible oil tanks – do not need to show the forward light).
- If the vessel or object is over 25 metres wide, an additional all-round white at or near each side.
- If it is over 100 metres long, additional all-round white lights, on the centre line if it is less than 25 metres wide, or down the sides if it is over 25 metres wide, so that adjacent lights are not more than 100 metres apart.

An inconspicuous or partly submerged object being towed by day, must show the day signal of a diamond shape, as specified above, even if the tow is less than 200 metres long. The diamond must be shown at or near the stern of the last object being towed. If the

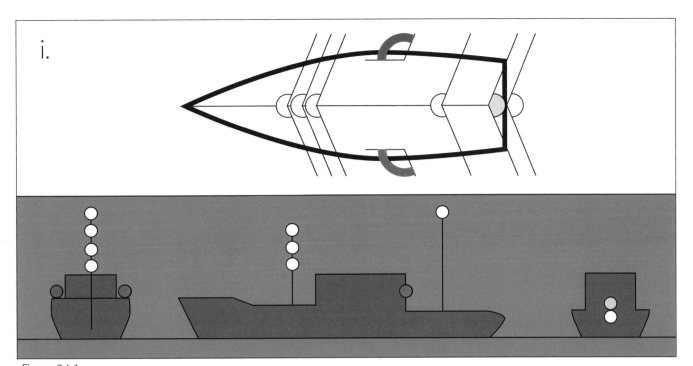

Figure 24.1

d. Tug over 50 metres (or possibly less) in length, with a tow more than 200 metres in length – i. or ii.

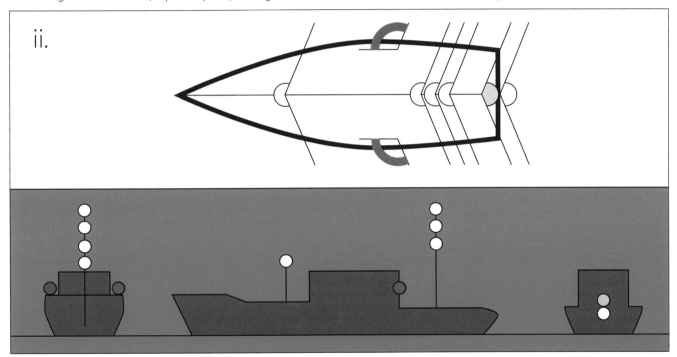

length of tow is over 200 metres, then an additional diamond must be shown as far forward on the towed object as possible.

The towing vessel will only display a diamond if the length of tow is more than 200 metres.

If it is impossible for the towed vessel or object to show the required lights or shapes, then the towing vessel must try to warn other vessels of the relationship of the tow, and its length. This could be done with a searchlight by night, or perhaps by means of a VHF radio.

> h. Where from any sufficient cause it is impracticable for a vessel or object being towed to exhibit the lights or shapes prescribed in Paragraph e. or g. of this Rule, all possible measures shall be taken to light the vessel or object towed or at least to indicate the presence of such vessel or object.

> i. Where from any sufficient cause it is impracticable for a vessel not normally engaged in towing operations to display the lights prescribed in Paragraph a. or c. of this Rule, such vessel shall not be required to exhibit those lights when engaged in towing another vessel in distress or otherwise in need

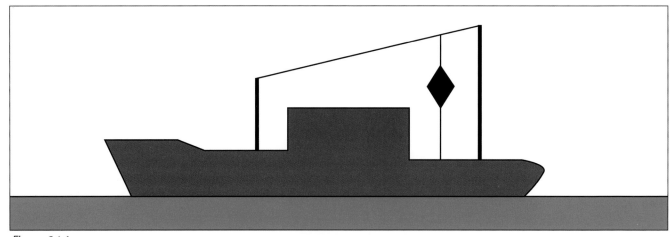

Figure 24.1
   e. *Tug by day, with tow more than 200 metres in length.*

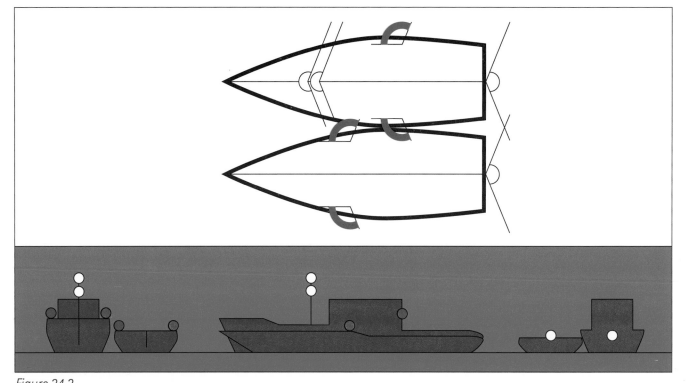

Figure 24.2
   a. *Tug less than 50 metres in length, towing alongside.*

of assistance. All possible measures shall be taken to indicate the nature of the relationship between the towing vessel and the vessel being towed as authorised by Rule 36 in particular to illuminate the towline.

If a vessel which is not fully equipped for towing undertakes a tow, perhaps to assist a distressed vessel, then it is exempted from having to show the lights and shapes required by the Rules. However, the towing vessel must warn other vessels of the fact that it is towing another vessel.

Rule 36 states that any signal to attract attention must be such that it cannot be mistaken for a manoeuvring signal, nor an aid to navigation.

Summary of Rule 24 – Towing and Pushing.

1. *A power-driven vessel when towing will show additional masthead lights, vertically above each other. There are two, if the length of the tow is 200 metres or less, and three if it exceeds 200 metres. These additional lights show through the same arc as the normal masthead lights, and can replace either the forward or the after masthead light of a normal power-driven vessel's lights.*

2. *When towing astern, the tug shows a yellow towing light above the stern light, showing through the same arc as the stern light. Some coastal states have local rules stipulating that this yellow towing light is shown when towing alongside and/or when pushing ahead.*

3. *By day, if the length of tow is less than 200 metres, the towing vessel shows no specific day signals. If the length*

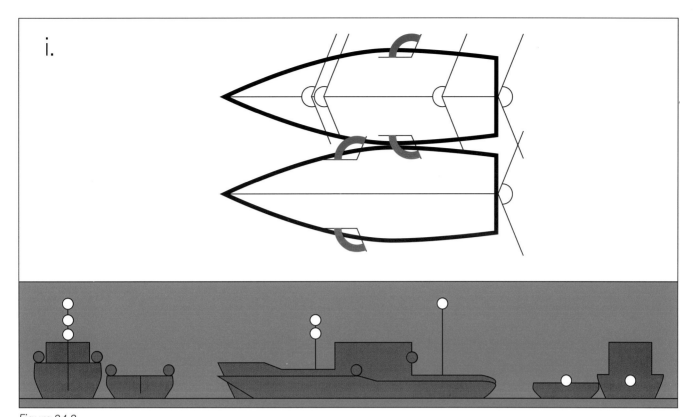

Figure 24.2

b. Tug more than 50 metres (or possibly less) in length, towing alongside i. or ii.

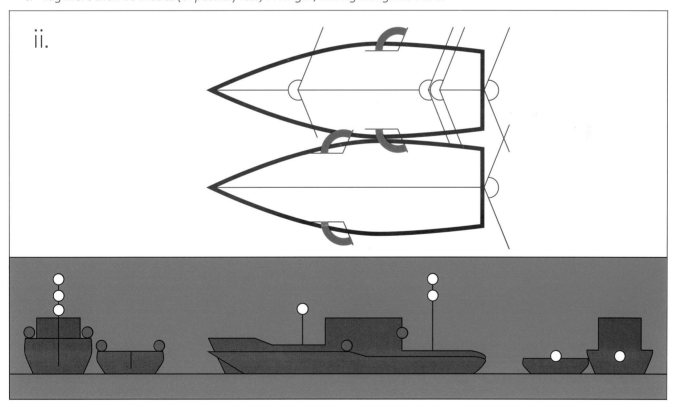

of tow (from stern of tug to stern of last vessel) exceeds 200 metres, then the tug shows a black diamond where it can best be seen, and a similar diamond is shown on the towed vessel.

4. If a vessel is pushing ahead as a rigid composite unit, then the unit is lit as a normal power-driven vessel.

5. Vessels towed astern or alongside must show sidelights and a stern light, and vessels being pushed ahead, sidelights.

6. An inconspicuous or partially submerged object is lit with:
   • An all-round white at each end, except that dracones do not need the forward light.
   • If it is more than 25 metres wide, an extra white all-round light on each side.

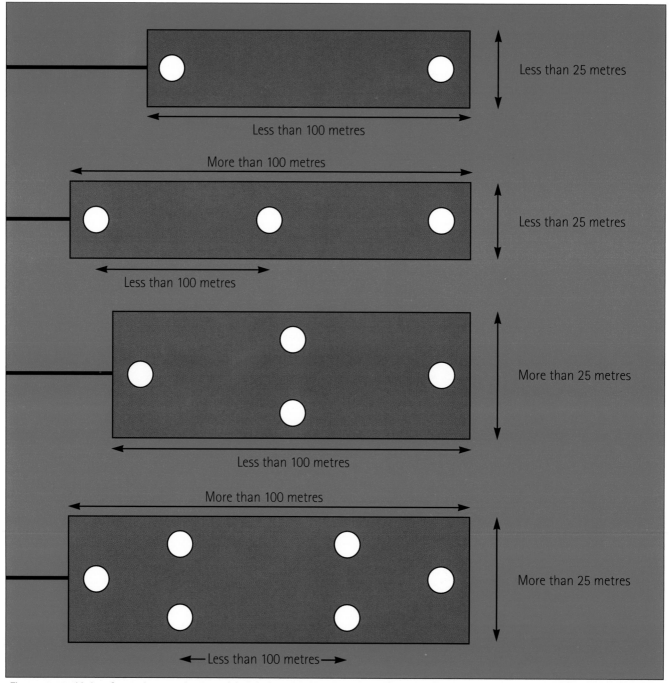

Figure 24.3 Lights for an inconspicuous object being towed.

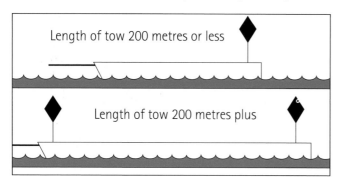

Figure 24.4 Day signal for an inconspicuous object being towed.

- *If it is more than 100 metres long, additional white lights so that adjacent lights are not more than 100 metres apart.*

- *By day, a diamond shall be shown on the stern of the object, and if the length of tow is more than 200 metres, then an additional diamond near the front of the towed object. The towing vessel only shows a diamond if the length of tow exceeds 200 metres.*

7. *If the lights or shapes cannot be shown by the tug or by the tow, then other vessels must be warned in a way that cannot be mistaken for being manoeuvring signals, distress signals or navigational aids.*

8. *Remember that showing the signals for a tug and tow grant no special privileges. If the tow severely hampers the towing vessel, then it must show the appropriate signals for Restricted in Ability to Manoeuvre – Rule 27.*

Rule 25. Sailing Vessels Underway and Vessels Under Oars

> a.   A sailing vessel underway shall exhibit:
> i.   sidelights;
> ii. a sternlight.

As with a power-driven vessel, the lights are to be shown whenever the vessel is underway, i.e. not aground, not at anchor nor made fast to the shore. Even if a sailing vessel is hove-to, she should still show the normal navigation lights, unless she is disabled through some exceptional circumstance, when she would be justified in showing the lights for not under command.

The normal lights are the same as the sidelights and stern light specified for a power-driven vessel. They must shine through the same arcs as specified for power-driven vessels, and must comply with the intensity specified in **Section 8** of **Annex I**, to give the visible distances specified in **Rule 22**:

- Vessels 50 metres or more – 3 miles for sidelights and stern light.
- Vessels 12 to 50 metres – 2 miles for sidelights and stern light.
- Vessels less than 12 metres – 1 mile for sidelights and 2 miles for stern light.

Remember that **Rule 21** told us that for a vessel under 20 metres, the sidelights could be combined in one lantern.

> b.   In a sailing vessel of less than 20 metres in length the lights prescribed in paragraph a. of this Rule may be combined in one lantern at or near the top of the mast where it can best be seen.

The single tri-coloured lantern at the masthead is limited to <u>sailing</u> vessels under 20 metres in length. Remember, that if there is an auxiliary engine being used to propell the vessel in addition to the sails, then the vessel ceases to be classed as a sailing vessel, and navigation lights for a power-driven vessel must be used. Any vessel less than 20 metres can combine the sidelights in a single lantern, but only a sailing vessel under 20 metres can combine all three lights at the masthead.

The advantage of the tri-coloured lantern is that being mounted on the top of the mast, it is less likely to be masked by the sails, and should be more visible from a distance than deck mounted navigation lights. It also reduces the power consumption to one bulb instead of three – a factor that could be important to a small yacht. However, it is important to remember to switch over to lower mounted lights when entering harbour, not only to comply with the Rule if motoring, but also nearby vessels could well miss seeing a masthead mounted light, which is likely to be above their field of vision.

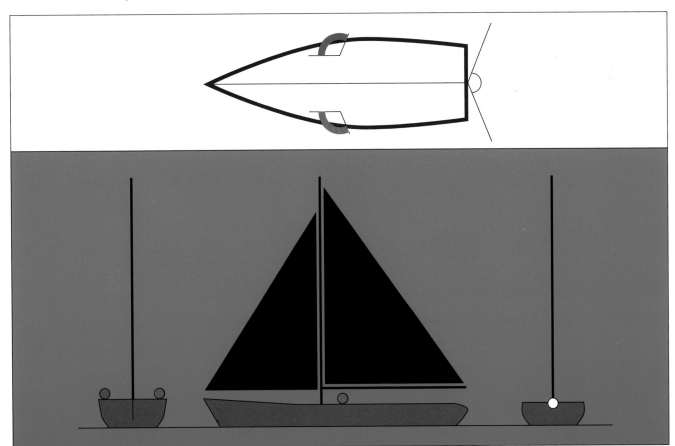

Figure 25.1 Navigation lights for a sailing vessel.
   a.   Any size of sailing vessel.

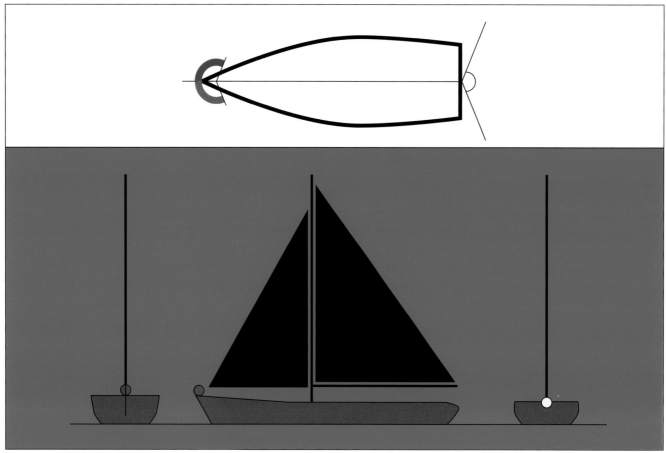

Figure 25.1 Navigation lights for a sailing vessel.
  b. Option for sailing vessels less than 20 metres in length.

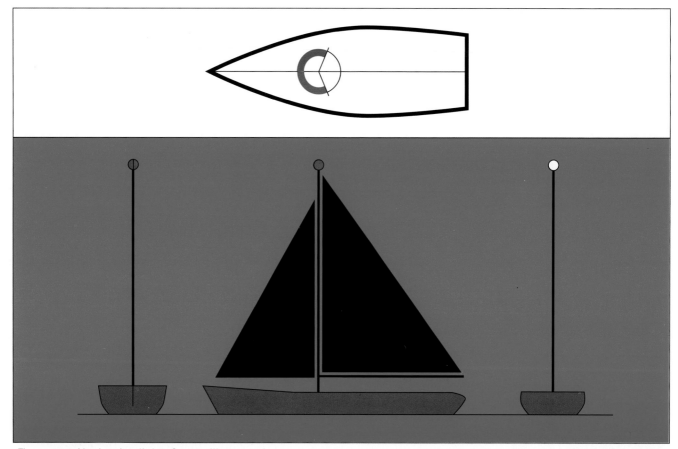

Figure 25.1 Navigation lights for a sailing vessel.
  c. Another option for sailing vessels less than 20 metres in length.

c.   A sailing vessel underway may, in addition to the lights prescribed in paragraph a. of this Rule, exhibit at or near the top of the mast, where they can best be seen, two all-round lights in a vertical line, the upper being red and the lower green, but these lights shall not be exhibited in conjunction with the combined (tri-coloured masthead) lantern permitted by paragraph b. of this Rule.

d.i.   A sailing vessel of less than 7 metres in length shall, if practicable, exhibit the lights prescribed in paragraph a. or b. of this Rule, but if she does not, she shall have ready at hand an electric torch or lighted lantern showing a white light which shall be exhibited in sufficient time to prevent collision.

Sailing vessels <u>may</u> show all-round red over green lights, at or near the top of the mast. It is obvious that if the red over green lights were shown at the same time as a masthead tri-colour, it could cause confusion. They should only be shown in conjunction with "normal" sidelights and stern light. These all-round red and green lights are to be shown only by sailing vessels, so they must be extinguished if the vessel is motor-sailing, or motoring.

Annex 1, Section 9 says that if all-round lights are to be shown, then there should not be dark sectors of more than 6°. A pair of lights can be used, suitably mounted and screened to appear as one, from a distance of one mile.

For what it is worth, I remember the lights as "Red over green help a sailboat be seen!"

This Rule does not give a blanket exemption to small sailing vessels to sail without navigation lights. It says that they <u>shall</u>, if practicable, show the prescribed lights. If it is deemed not practicable to show the correct lights, then a white light must be shown in time to prevent a collision.

ii.   A vessel under oars may exhibit the lights prescribed in this Rule for sailing vessels, but if she does not, she shall have ready at hand an electric torch or lighted lantern showing a white light which shall be exhibited in sufficient time to prevent collision.

Note the difference between the Rule for vessels being rowed and small sailing vessels. The vessel being rowed <u>may</u> show sidelights and a stern light, but if she chooses not to, then a white light must be available to be shown in time to avoid a collision.

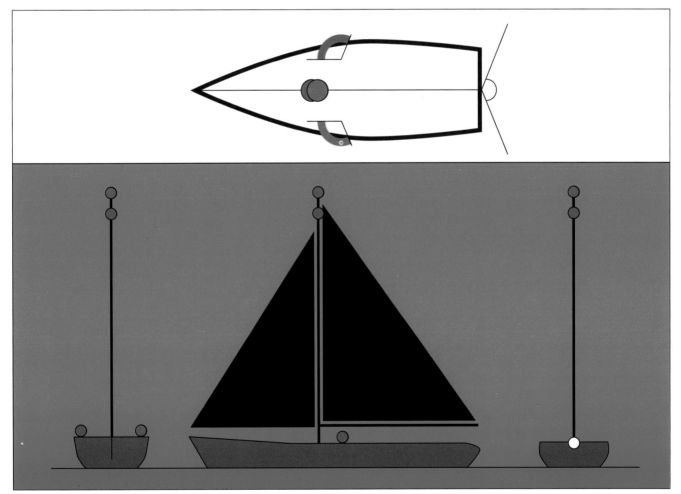

Figure 25.2 Optional all-round red and green lights for a sailing vessel.

> e.   A vessel proceeding under sail when also being propelled by machinery shall exhibit forward, where it can best be seen, a conical shape, apex downwards.

Whenever an auxiliary engine is being used to assist in the propulsion of the vessel, then the vessel ceases to be a sailing vessel, and it loses its privileges. To indicate the fact that it is a power-driven vessel, a vessel that is motor-sailing <u>shall</u> show a cone, apex down. Note that it is a "shall" not a "may". It is compulsory under the Rules to show such a cone when motor-sailing, and some coastal states will levy substantial fines for not doing so!

Annex 1 Section 6 defines the cone. It must be black, and have a base diameter of 0.6 metre, and a height of 0.6 metre. It allows that vessels of less than 20 metres in length can show a smaller size, **commensurate with the size of the vessel**.

To remember which way up the cone is displayed, I think of it as a **S**outh cone (as in a south cone for a gale warning, or as the south indication on a cardinal buoy), and a **S**outh cone indicates a **S**ailing vessel! We will see in **Rule 26** that a **N**orth cone indicates the direction of the **N**ets of a fishing vessel.

Summary of Rule 25 – Sailing Vessels.

1. *Sailing vessels over 7 metres <u>must</u> show sidelights and a stern light, whenever they are underway at night – even if they are not making way through the water. For any vessel less than 20 metres in length, the sidelights can be combined as a single lantern. For vessels less than 20 metres under sail, the sidelights and stern light may be combined in a masthead tri-colour lantern.*

2. *Visibility of the lights is 3 miles for vessels over 50 metres and 2 miles for vessels under 50 metres, except that the sidelights for vessels under 12 metres can be 1 mile.*

3. *Sailing vessels <u>may</u> show an all-round red light over an all-round green, (red over green help a sailboat be seen!) in addition to the "normal" sidelights and stern light. These all-round lights must not be shown in combination with "normal" sidelights, and must not be used in combination with a masthead tri-coloured light.*

4. *If under 7 metres in length, a sailing vessel <u>must</u> show sidelights and a stern light if practicable, but if not, then there must be a white light available to be shown in time to avoid a collision.*

5. *When a vessel is motor-sailing, then it ceases to be a sailing vessel, and must show the lights for a power-driven vessel of that size. By day, a vessel motor-sailing <u>must</u> show a cone, apex down. (South cone for a Sailing vessel). The cone is 0.6 metres base and height, except a vessel under 20 metres can show a smaller signal.*

6. *Vessels being rowed <u>may</u> show sidelights and stern light, but if not, must have a white light available to be shown in time to avoid a collision.*

Rule 26. Fishing Vessels

> a.   A vessel engaged in fishing, whether underway or at anchor, shall exhibit only the lights and shapes prescribed in this Rule.

Rule 3 defined a vessel engaged in fishing as one that is fishing with **nets, lines, trawls or other apparatus which restrict manoeuvrability, but does not include a vessel fishing with trolling lines or other fishing apparatus which do not restrict manoeuvrability**. So a yacht sailing along with a trolling line over the stern is not classed as a fishing vessel.

Any vessel which is classed as **engaged in fishing**, whether <u>at anchor</u> or <u>underway</u>, is required to show only the lights and shapes prescribed in this Rule. This means that a vessel fishing while at anchor must not show an anchor light – she must only show the lights of a fishing vessel. Nor can a vessel **engaged in fishing** be classed as "not under command", nor as "restricted in her ability to manoeuvre".

A trawler, by the nature of its equipment, cannot operate at anchor, so it will only be **vessels engaged in fishing other than trawling**, which are likely to be operating at anchor. We will see that such vessels, if they are operating at night, and have gear extending more than 150 metres, use an all-round white light to indicate the direction of the gear. If such a vessel were to show anchor lights as well, it would be very confusing.

> b.   A vessel when engaged in trawling, by which is meant the dragging through the water of a dredge net or other apparatus used as a fishing appliance, shall exhibit:
> i.   two all-round lights in a vertical line, the upper being green and the lower white, or a shape consisting of two cones with their apexes together in a vertical line, one above the other;
> ii.   a masthead light abaft of and higher than the all-round green light; a vessel of less than 50 metres in length shall not be obliged to exhibit such a light but may do so.
> iii. when making way through the water, in addition to the lights prescribed in this paragraph, sidelights and a sternlight.

The day signal for trawlers and, as we shall see in the next section, for other fishing vessels is the same – two black cones with the apexes together. The size of the cone is defined in **Annex 1 Section 6**, as 0.6 metres across the base and 0.6 metres in height. Vessels under 20 metres can show smaller signals, but the old signal of a basket in the rigging is no longer an acceptable alternative for small vessels. The signal should only be shown when the vessel is

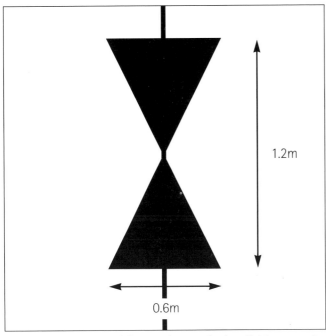

Figure 26.1 Day signal for trawlers and other fishing vessels.

same as the second masthead light required for a power-driven vessel of 50 metres or more. A trawler of <u>less than 50 metres may</u> show this white masthead light. This masthead light is shown at all times when the vessel is engaged in trawling, even if it is stopped in the water.

Note that because it is a "masthead light" it is <u>not</u> an all-round light. It shows through the normal arc of any other masthead light i.e. from 22.5° abaft the beam, through the bows, to 22.5° abaft the other beam. **Rule 22** tells us that the visibility of this masthead light must be 6 miles for a vessel over 50 metres in length; 20 to 50 metres long – 5 miles; 12 to 20 metres – 3 miles and under 12 metres – 2 miles.

If the vessel is **making way** through the water, then it must show the normal sidelights and stern lights. If it is stopped in the water, then these should be extinguished, leaving just the all-round lights, and, if carried, the after masthead light showing. Note that this is different from what is required of a power-driven vessel. A power-driven vessel must show the sidelights and stern light at all times when underway, regardless of whether it is making way or stopped in the water – **Rule 23**.

actually engaged in fishing, and not when going to or from the fishing grounds.

A vessel **engaged in trawling** shows an all-round green over white. Vessels engaged in other kinds of fishing, which could include surface nets, show red over white. The trawler, usually has her gear set deep in the water, which presents little danger to other vessels, so her lights are green over white. The more dangerous surface fishing vessels show red over white. (Green over white – trawler at night. Red over white – dangerous fishing boat at night!) **Rule 22** states that the visibility of these all-round lights must be 3 miles for a vessel over 50 metres, and 2 miles for those under 50 metres.

A trawler <u>over 50 metres must</u> carry a white masthead light abaft and above the all-round green light. This is the

c. A vessel engaged in fishing, other than trawling, shall exhibit:

i. two all-round lights in a vertical line, the upper being red and the lower white, or a shape consisting of two cones with their apexes together in a vertical line, one above the other;

ii. when there is outlying gear extending more than 150 metres horizontally from the vessel, an all-round white light or a cone apex upwards in the direction of the gear;

iii. when making way through the water, in addition to the lights prescribed in this paragraph, sidelights and a sternlight.

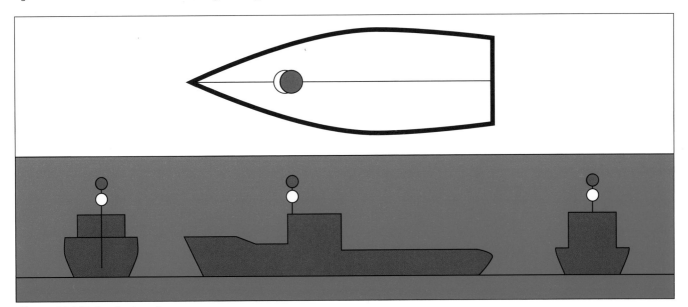

Figure 26.2 Lights for trawlers.
a. Trawler less than 50 metres in length, not making way through the water.

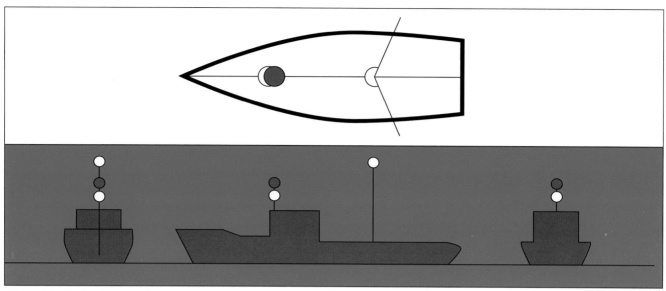

Figure 26.2 Lights for trawlers.
  b. *Trawler more than 50 metres (or possibly less) in length, not making way through the water.*

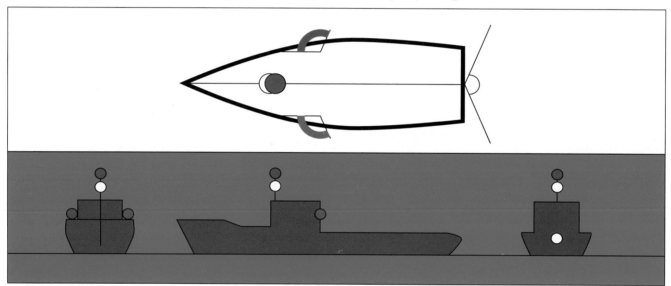

Figure 26.2 Lights for trawlers.
  c. *Trawler less than 50 metres in length, making way through the water.*

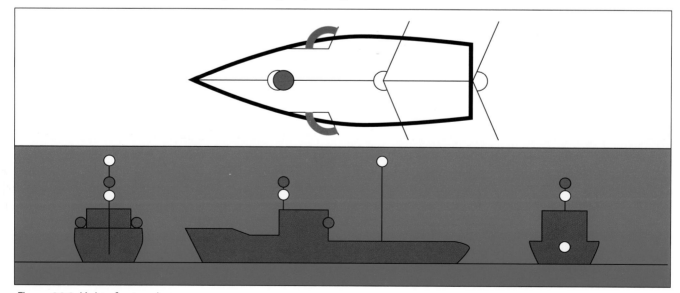

Figure 26.2 Lights for trawlers.
  d. *Trawler more than 50 metres (or possibly less) in length, making way through the water.*

In this section, when we use the term "fishing vessel", we mean a "vessel engaged in fishing other than trawling".

The day signal for a fishing vessel is the same as for a trawler – two black cones apexes together. The size of each cone is 0.6 metres for base and height, except that vessels under 20 metres may show smaller signals.

A fishing vessel often presents a greater danger to other vessels, especially if using gear near the surface, so her all-round lights are red (for danger) over white. (Red over white – dangerous fishing boat at night). The visibility of these lights is 3 miles for vessels over 50 metres and 2 miles for under 50 metres.

Notice that there is no mention of a second white masthead light as was required for trawlers over 50 metres and optional for smaller. This is because a fishing vessel

uses an all-round white light to indicate outlying gear that extends 150 metres or more from the vessel. This white light is set in the direction of the gear. If there were an additional white masthead light, it could cause confusion. **Annex 1, Section 4** specifies the positioning of this light. It must be at least 2 metres but not more than 6 metres from the red over white all-round lights. It must be lower than the all-round white, but higher than the sidelights.

By day, the presence of outlying gear, which extends 150 metres or more, is indicated by a cone, apex up, in the direction of the gear. (Apex up is a "north" cone. **N**orth cone – indicates **N**ets. Remember, the **S**outh cone indicated a **S**ailing vessel.)

When the fishing vessel is making way through the water, then she must show sidelights and a stern light, but

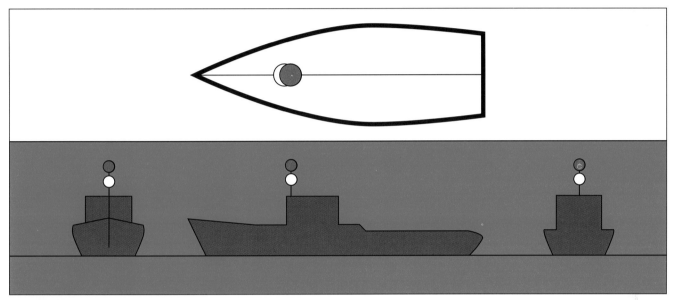

Figure 26.3 Lights for vessels engaged on fishing other than trawling.
   a. Fishing vessel (over or under 50 metres in length) stopped in the water, or fishing at anchor.

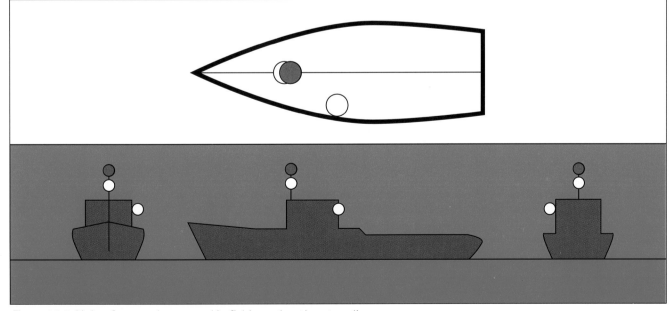

Figure 26.3 Lights for vessels engaged in fishing other than trawling.
   b. Fishing vessel (over or under 50 metres in length) stopped in the water, or fishing at anchor, with gear extending more than 150 metres on her port side.

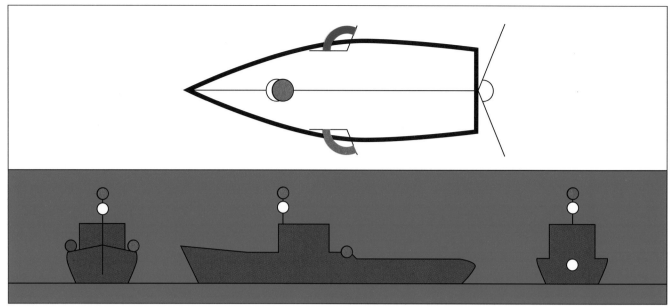

Figure 26.3 Lights for vessels engaged on fishing other than trawling.
*   c.   Fishing vessel (over or under 50 metres in length) making way.*

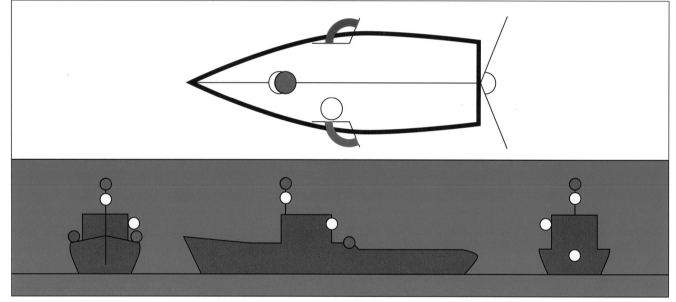

Figure 26.3 Lights for vessels engaged on fishing other than trawling.
*   d.   Fishing vessel (over or under 50 metres in length) making way, with gear extending more than 150 metres on her   port side.*

these must be turned off when she is stopped. Once again, remember that a "normal" power-driven vessel shows her sidelights and stern light at all times when she is underway, even if stopped in the water.

Trawlers and fishing vessels only show these signals while **engaged in fishing**. On their way to or from the fishing grounds they show only the normal lights of a power-driven vessel (unless of course they are under sail!), and would of course show two white masthead lights if they were over 50 metres in length.

> d.   The additional signals described in Annex II to these regulations apply to a vessel engaged in fishing in close proximity to other vessels engaged in fishing.

These signals are prescribed for trawlers and purse seiners. The lights are all-round lights, and they should be 0.9 metres apart. They should be shown at a lower level that the other all-round lights, and should have a visibility of at least one mile, but less than that of the other lights.

When fishing in close proximity to others, a trawler of 20 metres or more in length is required to show:
*   When shooting nets – two white lights in a vertical line;
*   When hauling nets – white over red in a vertical line (we will see later that this is the same signal for a pilot vessel);
*   When the nets are fast on an obstruction – two red lights in a vertical line.

When pair trawling, vessels over 20 metres must each direct a searchlight forward, and in the direction of the second vessel. When shooting or hauling their nets, or if the nets become fast on an obstruction, each should show the same lights as a single vessel would.

Vessels under 20 metres may show the above lights, but are not compelled to do so.

A vessel engaged in fishing with a purse seine net, if she is hampered by her gear, <u>may</u> show two all-round yellow lights in a vertical line. These flash alternately every second, with equal periods of light and dark (isophase).

Remember that **Rule 1** allows the **Government of Any State** to make special Rules. A coastal state may have special rules for vessels fishing in its waters, and require particular lights or signals to be shown. Any such rules would be given in a local pilot book.

> e. A vessel when not engaged in fishing shall not exhibit the lights or shapes prescribed in this Rule, but only those prescribed for a vessel of her length.

As we have already mentioned, the vessel <u>must be engaged in fishing</u> to be classed as a fishing vessel or trawler. When not engaged in fishing, she should not show any of the lights or shapes of a fishing vessel, but only those lights for a power-driven (or sailing!) vessel of her size.

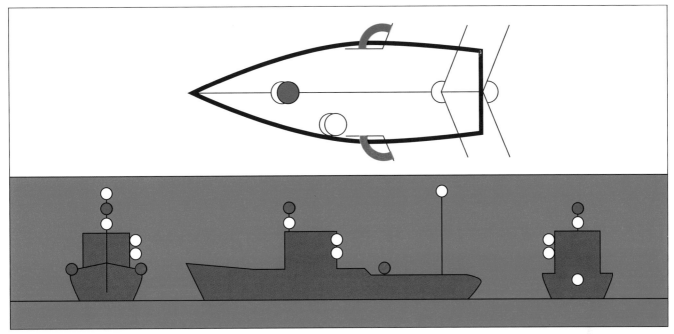

Figure 26.4 Lights for trawlers fishing in proximity to others.
   a. Trawler over 50 metres in length (or possibly less) shooting nets, making way through the water.

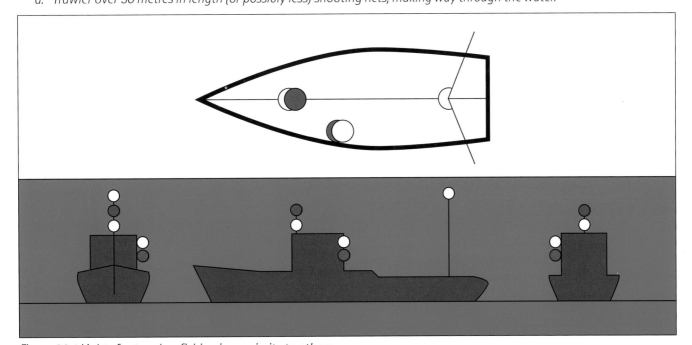

Figure 26.4 Lights for trawlers fishing in proximity to others.
   b. Trawler over 50 metres in length (or possibly less) hauling nets, stopped in the water.

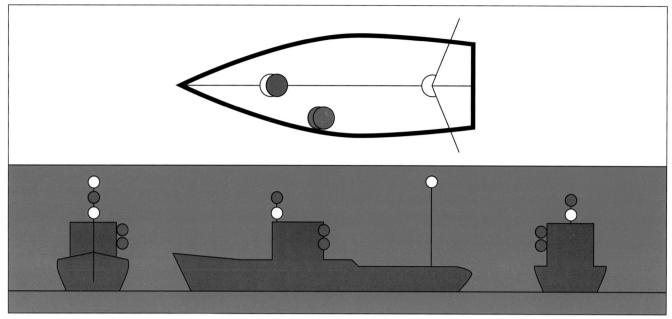

Figure 26.4 Lights for trawlers fishing in proximity to others.
c. *Trawler over 50 metres in length (or possibly less) with nets fast on an obstruction (obviously it will not be making way through the water!)*

Summary of Rule 26 – Fishing Vessels.

1. *A vessel must be <u>engaged in fishing</u> to be classed as a fishing vessel, otherwise she is classed as a normal power-driven or sailing vessel, and the fishing signals must not be shown.*
2. *If engaged in fishing, then the vessel only shows the lights prescribed in this Rule, and no others – she does not show an anchor light, and cannot be classed as not under command nor restricted in her ability to manoeuvre while showing the fishing signals.*
3. *A **trawler** shows green over white all-round lights, (Green over white – trawler at night), and if over 50 metres it <u>must</u> show a white masthead light abaft of, and above the green light, even if not making way. A trawler under 50 metres <u>may</u> show this light.*
   - *When <u>making way</u>, it must also show sidelights and stern light.*
   - *Day signal is two black cones with apexes together – cones 0.6 metres across base and 0.6 metres high.*
4. *A **fishing vessel** other than a trawler shows red over white all-round lights, (Red over white – fishing boat at night. Red for danger of surface nets), and does not show a white masthead light while fishing, regardless of size.*
   - *When <u>making way</u>, it must also show sidelights and stern light.*
   - *Day signal is the same as for a trawler – two black cones, apexes together – cones 0.6 metres across base and 0.6 metres high.*
   - *If the fishing vessel has gear extending more than 150 metres, it then shows an all-round white, or a cone, point up (**N**orth cone for **N**ets) in the direction of the gear.*

5. *When fishing in close proximity to others, a trawler of 20 metres or more in length is required to show:*
   - *When shooting nets – two white lights in a vertical line.*
   - *When hauling nets – white over red in a vertical line (we will see later that this is the same signal for a pilot vessel).*
   - *When the nets are fast on an obstruction – two red lights in a vertical line.*
6. *Pair trawlers must use searchlights to indicate their nets, in addition to showing the above lights.*
7. *Vessels fishing with a purse seine net show two all-round yellow lights which flash alternately every second when she is hampered by her gear.*

Rule 27. Vessels not under command or restricted in their ability to manoeuvre

a. A vessel not under command shall exhibit:
i. two all-round red lights in a vertical line where they can best be seen;
ii. two balls or similar shapes in a vertical line where they can best be seen;
iii. when making way through the water, in addition to the lights prescribed in this paragraph, sidelights and a sternlight. (Note – no masthead lights).

Rule 3 told us that a vessel not under command was one which **through some exceptional circumstance is unable to manoeuvre as required by these Rules, and is**

therefore unable to keep out of the way of another vessel. The vessel must be underway (i.e. not at anchor, not aground nor made fast to the shore), but not necessarily making way through the water. If it is making way, then it must show the normal sidelights and stern light in addition to the two all-round red lights which signify not under command. While the red lights for not under command are displayed, white masthead lights are not shown, regardless of whether the vessel is making way or not, because if they were shown, the vessel could be mistaken for one showing the signal that it was aground, (two red all-round lights and the anchor lights for a vessel of that particular size – **Rule 30**).

By day, the two red lights are replaced by two black balls, in a vertical line. **Annex 1 Section 6** states that they must be 0.6 metres in diameter and 1.5 metres apart. Vessels less than 20 metres can display smaller shapes.

b.   A vessel restricted in her ability to manoeuvre, except a vessel engaged in mine clearance operations, shall exhibit;

i.   three all-round lights in a vertical line where they can best be seen. The highest and lowest of these lights shall be red and the middle light shall be white;

ii.   three shapes in a vertical line where they can best be seen. The highest and lowest of these shapes shall be balls and the middle one a diamond;

iii.   when making way through the water, a masthead light or lights, sidelights and a sternlight, in addition to the lights prescribed in sub-paragraph i.;

iv.   when at anchor, in addition to the lights or shapes prescribed in sub-paragraphs i. and ii., the light, lights or shapes prescribed in Rule 30.

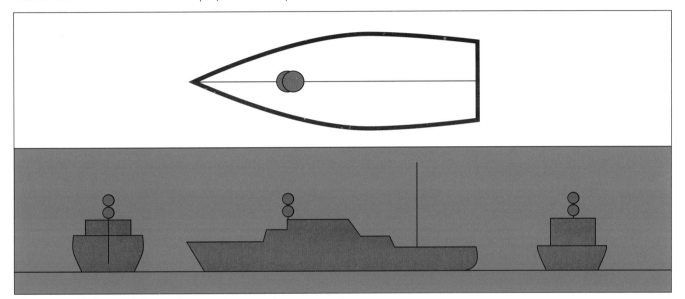

Figure 27.1 Lights and shapes for vessels not under command.
  a. Vessel not under command, stopped in the water.

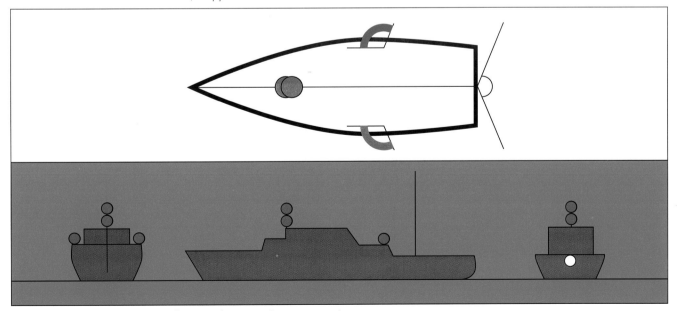

Figure 27.1 Lights and shapes for vessels not under command.
  b. Vessel not under command, making way.

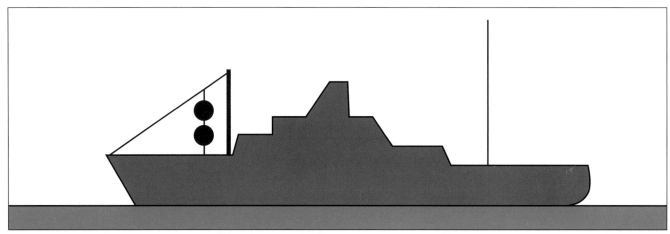

Figure 27.1 Lights and shapes for vessels not under command.
  c. Day shape for vessel not under command, either making way or stopped in the water.

Rule 3 defined a vessel to be restricted in her ability to manoeuvre when **from the nature of her work** (the vessel) **is restricted in her ability to manoeuvre as required by these Rules, and is therefore unable to keep out of the way of another vessel**. The definition included, but was not limited to:

- Vessels laying, servicing or picking up a navigation mark, submarine cable or pipeline;
- Vessels engaged in dredging, surveying or underwater operations;
- Vessels engaged in replenishment or transferring persons, provisions or cargo while underway;
- Vessels engaged in launching or recovering aircraft;
- Vessels with a tow which severely restricts the towing vessel and the tow in their ability to deviate from their course.

It also includes minesweepers, but as we shall see, they have their own signals.

The signal for restricted in ability to manoeuvre is three all-round lights in a row – red over white over red. When making way, the vessel must show sidelights, stern light and masthead light or lights as appropriate to her size. (She must show two masthead lights if over 50 metres in length, and if less than 50 metres, she can show either one, or two, masthead lights). As with vessels not under command, the sidelights, stern light, and in this case masthead lights are shown only when the vessel is making way through the water, unlike a power-driven vessel which must show the lights at all times when it is underway, even if stopped in the water.

The day signal is three black shapes – a ball over a diamond over a ball. (The balls replace the red lights, and the diamond replaces the white.) **Annex 1 Section 6** specifies the balls as being 0.6 metres in diameter, and the diamond to be made of two cones base-to-base, each with a diameter of 0.6 metres and a height of 0.6 metres i.e. the height of the diamond is 1.2 metres. Vessels smaller than 20 metres are allowed to show smaller signals.

If operating at anchor, then **Section iv** states that the anchor signals of **Rule 30** must be shown in addition to these signals. The anchor signals are a black ball by day (0.6 metres in diameter), shown in the forward part of the vessel, and by night, an all-round white in the forward part, and, if over 50 metres, a second all-round white light in the after part of the vessel, lower than the forward light.

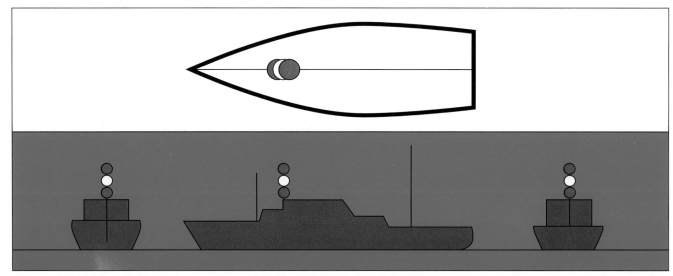

Figure 27.2 Lights and shapes for vessels restricted in their ability to manoeuvre.
  a. Vessel restricted in her ability to manoeuvre, under way but not making way through the water.

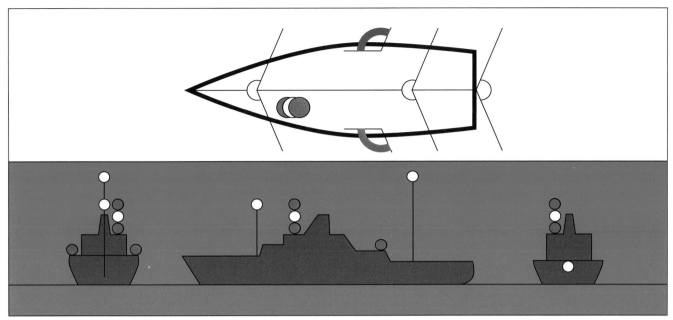

Figure 27.2 Lights and shapes for vessels restricted in their ability to manoeuvre.
  b. Vessel over 50 metres (or possibly less) in length, restricted in her ability to manoeuvre, making way through the water.

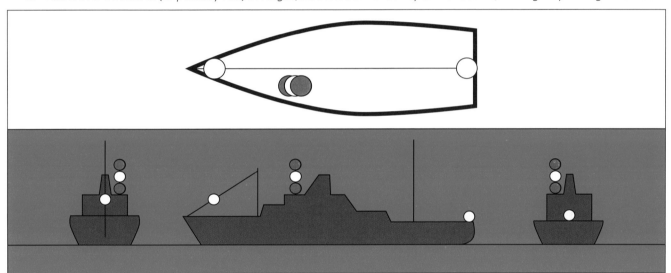

Figure 27.2 Lights and shapes for vessels restricted in their ability to manoeuvre.
  c. Vessel over 50 metres (or possibly less) in length, restricted in her ability to manoeuvre, operating at anchor.

If the vessel is at anchor, then it cannot be transferring people or provisions under way, it cannot be towing a tow which severely restricts its ability to deviate from its course, and it is unlikely to be launching or recovering aircraft, which is usually done underway. So a vessel which is showing the signals for restricted in her ability to manoeuvre, and the signals showing it is at anchor, is likely to be engaged in servicing, picking up or laying navigation marks, submarine cables or pipelines, or to be engaged in dredging, surveying or underwater operations.

We shall see in **Section d.** of this Rule that a vessel engaged in dredging or underwater operations, when restricted in her ability to manoeuvre, has an extra signal to show if there is an obstruction on one side. When showing this signal, she does not show the anchor signals, even if she is operating at anchor.

c. A power-driven vessel engaged in a towing operation such as severely restricts the towing vessel and her tow in their ability to deviate from their course shall, in addition to the lights or shapes prescribed in Rule 24 a., exhibit the lights or shapes prescribed in sub-paragraphs b. i. and ii. of this Rule.

Rule 24 stipulated that a vessel with a tow shows two white masthead lights in a vertical row, or three if the tow is more than 200 metres long, in place of either the forward or after masthead light of a power-driven vessel. In addition to the sidelights and stern light, it also shows a yellow towing light above the stern light, showing through the same arc. By day, if the tow is over 200 metres long, then the towing vessel and the towed vessel show a black diamond.

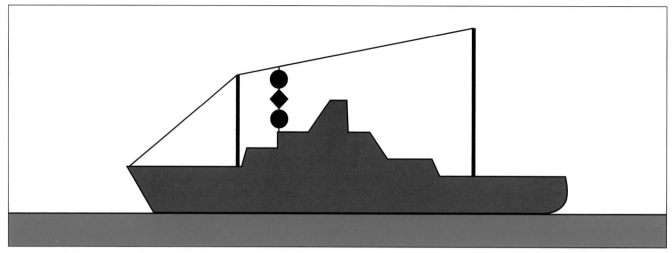

Figure 27.3 Day shapes for vessels restricted in their ability to manoeuvre.
a. Vessel restricted in her ability to manoeuvre, either making way or stopped in the water.

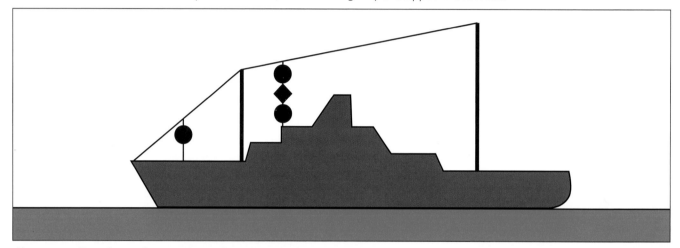

Figure 27.3 Day shapes for vessels restricted in their ability to manoeuvre.
b. Vessel restricted in her ability to manoeuvre, operating at anchor.

If the size or nature of the tow, or indeed the weather or other conditions are such that it **severely restricts the towing vessel and her tow in their ability to deviate from their course**, the towing vessel shows the signals for restricted in her ability to manoeuvre. That is, the white over red over white all-round lights by night, and the ball over diamond over ball by day. No extra signals are shown by the towed vessel, only the diamond, if the length of tow exceeds 200 metres.

When the towing vessel is showing the signals for restricted in her ability to manoeuvre, then Rule 18 – Responsibilities between vessels – states that other power-driven vessels, sailing vessels and vessels engaged in fishing must all keep out of her way. If the towing vessel is not showing the signal for restricted in her ability to manoeuvre, then, as far as the Rules are concerned, she receives no special privileges.

> d. A vessel engaged in dredging or underwater operations, when restricted in her ability to manoeuvre, shall exhibit the lights and shapes prescribed in sub-paragraphs b. i., ii. and iii. of this

> Rule (b.i. is the red-over-white-over red lights. b.ii. is the ball-diamond-ball day signal and b.iii. are the masthead light or lights, sidelights and stern light if making way) and shall in addition, when an obstruction exists, exhibit:
> i. two all-round red lights or two balls in a vertical line to indicate the side on which the obstruction exists;
> ii. two all-round green lights or two diamonds in a vertical line to indicate the side on which another vessel may pass;
> iii. when at anchor the lights or shapes prescribed in this paragraph instead of the lights or shape prescribed in Rule 30 (signals for vessels at anchor).

When a vessel is engaged in dredging or underwater operations which restrict her ability to manoeuvre, we have already seen that she should show red-over-white-over-red all-round lights at night, and the ball-diamond-ball by day. If there is an obstruction on one side, the vessel <u>shall</u> in addition show two all-round red lights in a vertical line, or two balls in a vertical line, on the side where the

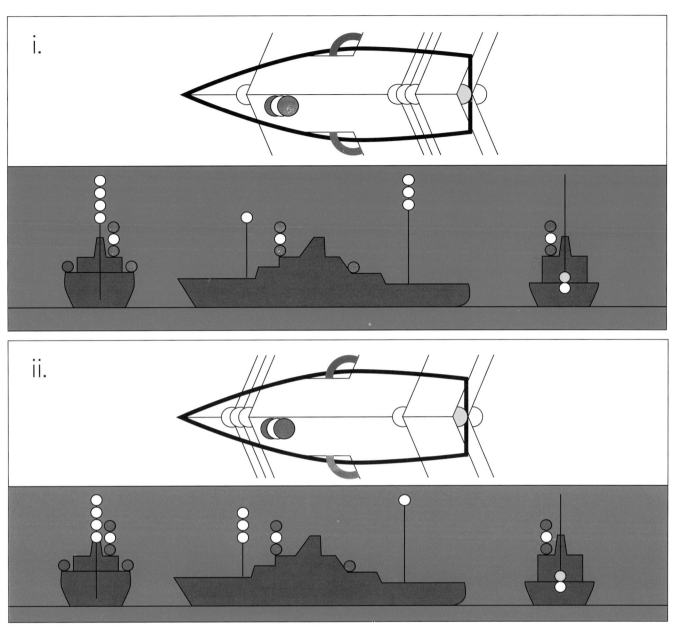

Figure 27.4 Lights for a vessel with a tow which restricts her ability to manoeuvre.
   Vessel over 50 metres (or possibly less), with a tow of more than 200 metres in length, which restricts her ability to manoeuvre. i. or ii.

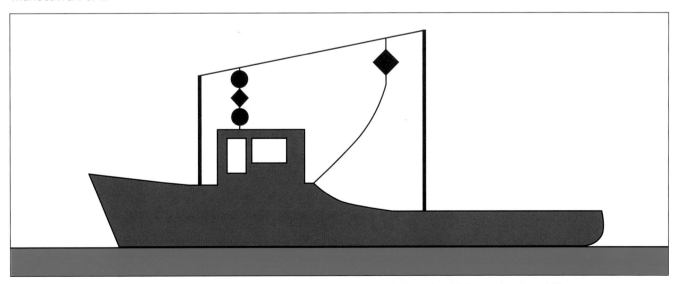

Figure 27.5 Day shapes for a vessel with a tow of more than 200 metres in length which restricts her ability to manoeuvre.

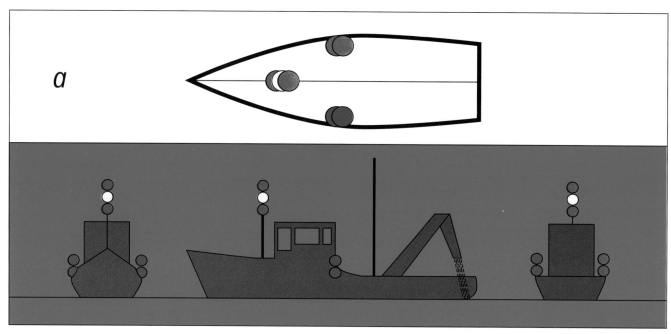

Figure 27.6 Vessel engaged in dredging or underwater operations, restricted in her ability to manoeuvre, with an obstruction on her starboard side.

    a. By night.   b. By day.

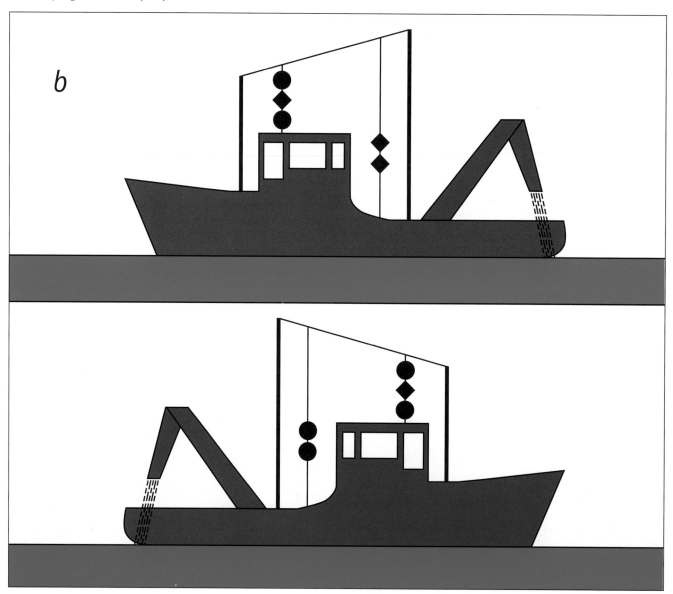

obstruction exists. In addition, she <u>shall</u> show two all-round green lights in a vertical line, or two diamonds by day, to indicate the side on which it is safe for other vessels to pass. (Note that a diamond day signal normally replaces a white light, but in this case, the diamonds are replacing green lights.)

Annex 1 Section 4 stipulate that these lights or shapes must be shown as far horizontally as is practicable from the red-white-red or ball-diamond-ball signals. The horizontal distance must be at least 2 metres, and the pairs of lights must be lower than the lowest of the three lights or shapes or the restricted in ability to manoeuvre signal. **Section 6** stipulates that the balls must be 0.6 metres in diameter, and the diamond 0.6 metres diameter and 1.2 metres high.

These vessels do not show the signal or lights of vessels at anchor, just the lights and shapes stipulated in this Rule.

> e. Whenever the size of a vessel engaged in diving operations makes it impracticable to exhibit all lights and shapes prescribed in paragraph d. of this Rule, the following shall be exhibited:
> i. three all-round lights in a vertical line where they can best be seen. The highest and lowest of these lights shall be red and the middle light shall be white;
> ii. a rigid replica of the International Code Flag "A" not less than 1 metre in height. Measures shall be taken to ensure its all-round visibility.

Annex 1, Section 6 allows that any vessel under 20 metres may show signals smaller than the stipulated sizes, so probably any vessel under 20 metres could be justified in adopting this paragraph.

Although the rigid replica of Code Flag "A" – white and blue halves, vertically separated, with a swallowtail on the blue fly is the stipulated signal for underwater operations, remember that **Rule 1** allows Coastal States to promulgate their own Rules. In many areas of the world, the signal for a vessel engaged in diving operations is a red flag, with a white diagonal cross. Whichever signal is being used, it should only be shown when diving operations are being carried out. The signal should not be shown while the vessel is *en-route* to or from the diving site.

> f. A vessel engaged in mine clearance operations shall in addition to the lights prescribed for a power-driven vessel in Rule 23 or to the lights or shape prescribed for a vessel at anchor in Rule 30 as appropriate, exhibit three all-round green lights or three balls. One of these lights or shapes shall be exhibited near the foremast head and one at each end of the fore yard. These lights or shapes indicate that it is dangerous for another vessel to approach within 1000 metres of the mine clearance vessel.

Vessels engaged in mine clearance operations are required to show special signals. These are three black balls, or three green lights arranged in a triangle. Normally the black ball of a day signal is represented by a red light at night, but in the case of a minesweeper, the lights are green.

Even though the obstruction may only exist on one side, other vessels are required to keep at least 1,000 metres clear in all directions.

If a minesweeper is underway at night, then it is required to show the sidelights, stern light and masthead light or lights of a power-driven vessel, even if it is stopped in the water. If it is operating at anchor, then it must show the appropriate signals required by Rule 30 – black ball by day, and all round white light or lights at night, in addition to the three balls or green lights.

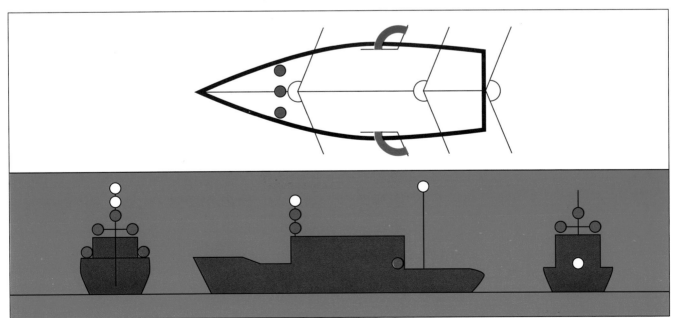

Figure 27.7
   a. Lights for a vessel engaged in mine clearance operations.

Figure 27.7

b. *Day shapes for a vessel engaged in mine clearance operations.*

> g.   Vessels of less than 12 metres in length, except those engaged in diving operations shall not be required to exhibit the lights and shapes prescribed in this Rule.

Vessels less than 12 metres in length do not have to carry lights or shapes to signify not under command, nor restricted in ability to manoeuvre. All vessels more than 12 metres are supposed to carry them, but if the vessel is under 20 metres, the shapes do not have to be of the size specified in Annex 1, they can be smaller.

Small vessels engaged in diving operations must show suitable signals. Paragraph e. of this Rule states that they can show a rigid replica of Code Flag "A" by day, but must still show the red-over white-over-red lights by night.

> h.   The signals prescribed in this Rule are not signals of vessels in distress and requiring assistance. Such signals are contained in Annex IV to these Regulations.

A vessel indicating that it is not under command is not in distress, and is not seeking assistance. It is warning other vessels that it cannot manoeuvre because of some "exceptional" circumstance, and other vessels should keep clear.

Summary of Rule 27 – Vessels not under command or restricted in their ability to manoeuvre.

1. *A vessel not under command shows two black balls by*

day, or two red lights by night. If it is <u>making way</u>, it shows sidelights and stern light, but not masthead lights – if the white masthead lights were shown it could make the vessel look as if it was showing the signals for being aground.

2. *A vessel cannot be "not under command" at anchor – that is the signal for being aground.*

3. *A vessel not under command is not in distress, and is not asking for assistance.*

4. *A vessel restricted in her ability to manoeuvre, except for those vessels engaged in mine clearance, must show ball-diamond-ball by day and red-white-red all-round lights at night. Vessels restricted in ability to manoeuvre include:*

   - *Vessels laying, servicing or picking up a navigation mark, submarine cable or pipeline;*
   - *Vessels engaged in dredging, surveying or underwater operations;*
   - *Vessels engaged in replenishment or transferring persons, provisions or cargo while underway;*
   - *Vessels engaged in launching or recovering aircraft;*
   - *Vessels with a tow which severely restricts the towing vessel and the tow in their ability to deviate from their course.*

9. *When <u>making way</u>, a vessel restricted in her ability to manoeuvre must also show the sidelights, stern light and masthead light or lights of a power-driven vessel.*

6. *If operating at anchor, then vessels restricted in their ability to manoeuvre must also show the appropriate anchor signals, black ball by day, and all-round light or lights at night (Rule 30). However, vessels dredging, or engaged in underwater operations where an obstruction exists on one side, must show two red lights or two black balls on the obstructed side, and two diamonds or two green lights on the safe side. When showing these signals, such a vessel does not then show the anchor signals.*

7. *Vessels under 20 metres may show smaller signals and vessels under 12 metres are exempt from carrying the signals at all, except that small vessels engaged in diving operations must show a rigid replica of Code Flag "A" at least 1 metre high, and must show the red-white-red lights at night.*

Rule 28. Vessels constrained by their draught

> A vessel constrained by her draught may, in addition to the lights prescribed for power-driven vessels in Rule 23, exhibit where they can best be seen three all-round red lights in a vertical line or a cylinder.

Rule 3 stated that a vessel constrained by its draught must be a power-driven vessel, which, because of her draught in relation to the available depth and <u>width</u> of navigable water, is severely restricted in her ability to deviate from the course she is following.

Notice that the Rule says that a vessel constrained by

her draught <u>may</u> display the signal – there is no obligation to do so, but obviously if she is not displaying the signal, she cannot expect the privileges of **Rule 18** to be granted. **Rule 18** stated that all vessels, except those not under command or restricted in their ability to manoeuvre

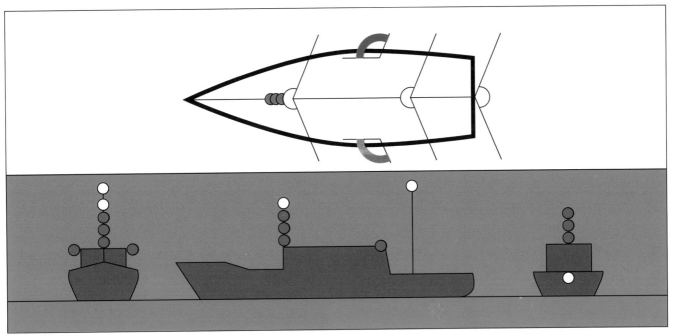

Figure 28.1 Lights and shapes for a vessel constrained by her draught, showing alternative positions for the lights.

must, as far as possible, avoid impeding the passage of a vessel which is constrained by her draught, which is <u>exhibiting the signals in Rule 28</u>.

The signals are three all-round red lights in a vertical line by night, or a black cylinder by day. **Annex 1 Section 2** says that if the lights cannot be carried below the masthead lights, then they may be shown above the after masthead light, or suspended between the after and fore masts. They must be within 2 metres of the centreline of the vessel. Section 6 says that the cylinder must be at least 0.6 metres in diameter, and the height must be twice the diameter.

The normal sidelights, stern light and masthead lights must be shown in addition to the three red lights.

Summary of Rule 28 – Vessels constrained by their draught.

1. A vessel constrained by her draught <u>may</u> show three red lights in a vertical row, or a black cylinder (at least 0.6 metres diameter, with a height of twice the diameter). Remember that it is the <u>width</u> of the navigable channel available to the vessel as much as the absolute depth of the channel, which determines if a vessel is constrained.

2. If the vessel does not show the signals, she cannot expect to be granted the privileges of Rule 18.

Rule 29. Pilot Vessels

> a.   A vessel engaged in pilotage duty shall exhibit:
> i.   at or near the masthead, two all-round lights in a vertical line, the upper being white and the lower red;
> ii.   when underway, in addition, sidelights and a sternlight;
> iii.   when at anchor, in addition to the lights prescribed in subparagraph i., the light, lights or shape prescribed in Rule 30 for vessels at anchor.

A pilot vessel, regardless of whether it is a power-driven vessel or a sailing vessel, shows two all-round lights near the masthead. They are white over red. I used to remember this as "White over red – pilot ahead", but then a friend told me that when a pilot comes climbing up the ladder to get on board, as his head clears the rail, the first thing that you see

is his white hat on top of his very red face – white over red!

When the vessel is underway, i.e. not at anchor, not aground nor made fast to the shore, she must show sidelights and a stern light. Note that she need not be making way through the water.

When the pilot vessel is showing the white over red signals, she does not show any masthead lights.

When at anchor, she must show the normal anchor signals of **Rule 30** – black ball by day, and all-round white light or lights by night. If she is on duty, then she will continue to show the white over red all-round lights.

> b.   A pilot vessel when not engaged on pilotage duty shall exhibit the lights or shapes prescribed for a similar vessel of her length.

When a pilot vessel is not on duty, she ceases to be classed as a pilot vessel, so she should not show the white over red lights. When at anchor she would show the normal signals required by **Rule 30** (black ball by day, and all-

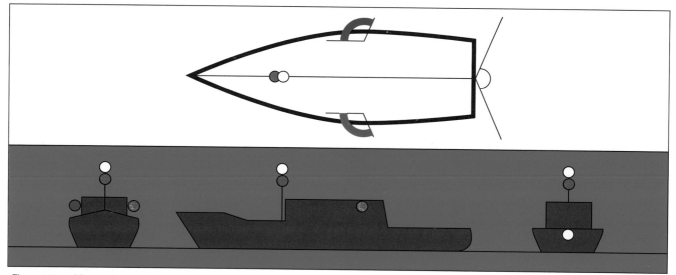

Figure 29.1 Lights for a pilot vessel.
   a. Pilot vessel under way, but not necessarily making way through the water.

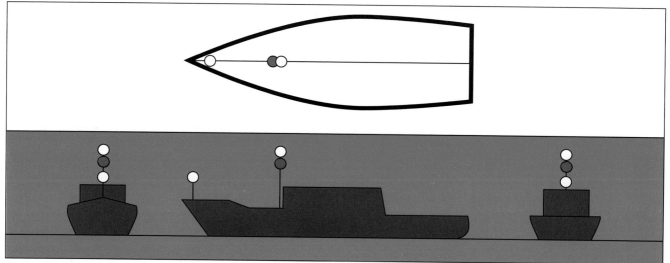

Figure 29.1 Lights for a pilot vessel.
   b. Pilot vessel on duty at anchor. (Compare with pilot vessel underway, seen from astern).

round white light or lights at night.) When underway, she would be lit as a normal power-driven vessel (unless of course she was a sailing pilot vessel!), and show sidelights, stern light and masthead light or lights.

There is no day signal or shape specified for Pilot Vessels in the Rules, but remember that Rule 1 allows Coastal States to make up their own Rules. A very common signal is a flag, divided horizontally, showing white over red.

International Code Flag "H", red and white in vertical halves, with the red at the fly, is the signal shown when a vessel has a pilot on board. Code flag "G", yellow and blue vertical stripes, is the signal to be shown when requesting a pilot.

Summary of Rule 29 – Pilot Vessels.

1. *Pilot vessels, when on duty, show white over red all-round lights at or near the masthead. (Remember the pilot's white hat on top of his red face as he clambers over the rail!)*
2. *When underway, but not necessarily making way, she shows sidelights and stern light, but no other masthead lights.*
3. *At anchor she shows the normal anchor lights for a vessel of her size, but continues to show the white over red all-round lights if she is on duty.*
4. *When not on duty, a pilot vessel does not show the white over red lights, and is lit as a power-driven (or sailing) vessel of her size.*
5. *No day signal is specified in the Rules, but a common signal stipulated by many Coastal States is a flag, divided horizontally, white over red.*

Rule 30. Anchored Vessels and Vessels Aground

A vessel is deemed to be at anchor when her anchor is set and holding. If the anchor is dragging, then the vessel is considered to be underway, and as such, she has to keep clear of other vessels which are anchored.

A vessel made fast to a mooring buoy is considered to be anchored.

> a. A vessel at anchor shall exhibit where it can best be seen:
> i. in the fore part, an all-round white light or one ball;
> ii. at or near the stern and at a lower level than the light prescribed in sub-paragraph i., an all-round white light.

Annex 1 specifies that the anchor ball must be 0.6 metres in diameter, except that vessels smaller than 20 metres may use a smaller size. The ball must be displayed in the forward part of the vessel by day.

Annex 1 also specifies the positioning of the anchor light or lights. If a second all-round light is shown, (which it must be if the vessel is over 50 metres) it must be placed near the stern, and it must be lower than the light shown forward. This arrangement of lights is the opposite of the arrangement of white masthead lights on a power-driven vessel, where the lower light is forward of the higher one.

> b. A vessel of less than 50 metres in length may exhibit an all-round white light where it can best be seen instead of the lights prescribed in paragraph a. of this Rule.

A vessel of less than 50 metres can show just a single white all-round light, and it does not necessarily have to be set in the forward part of the vessel. If the vessel displays two lights, then one must be in the forward part of the vessel, with the second one in the after part of the vessel. The after one must be lower than the forward one.

When choosing where to show a single all-round white anchor light, give some thought as to how visible it will be to approaching vessels. A light at the top of the mast of a yacht will be visible from a considerable distance, but may

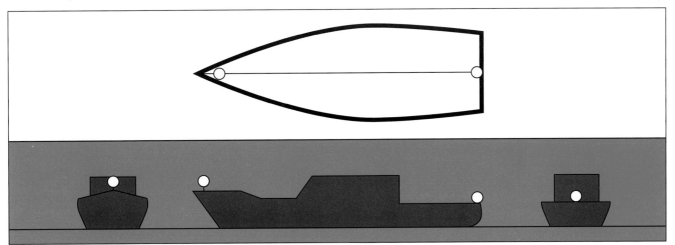

Figure 30.1 Lights for vessels at anchor.
Vessel over 50 metres in length (or possibly less). Note that the forward light is higher than the after one.

well be overlooked by vessels close at hand, which are the ones most likely to hit you! A light displayed at or near eye level for approaching vessels will be more readily noticed than one high above, on top of a mast.

> c.   A vessel at anchor may, and a vessel of 100 metres and more in length shall, also use the available working or equivalent lights to illuminate her decks.

Vessels over 100 metres in length are required to use their decklights to make themselves more conspicuous when at anchor at night. Smaller vessels may use their decklights if they wish. Such lights must be turned off as soon as the vessel gets underway, i.e. as soon as the anchor breaks out, or the mooring is let go.

> d.   A vessel aground shall exhibit the lights prescribed in paragraph a. or b. of this Rule and in

addition, where they can best be seen:
i.   two all-round red lights in a vertical line;
ii.   three balls in a vertical line.

The signal for a vessel aground combines the signals for being at anchor and not under command. At night the vessel aground will show the anchor light or lights required (two must be shown if she is over 50 metres) and the two all-round red lights in a vertical line of not under command.

Note that two red lights in a vertical line, and a single white could be a vessel under 50 metres aground, or it could be a vessel not under command, making way, seen from astern.

By day, the signal is three black balls in a vertical line. This may at first appear to be a little confusing that the <u>two</u> red lights are replaced by <u>three</u> black balls. However, it really is the same as the signals for being at anchor (one

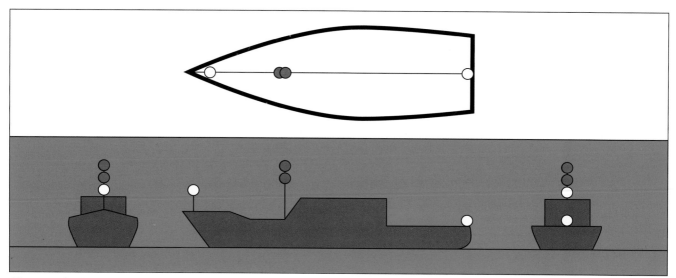

Figure 30.2 Lights for vessels aground.
  a. Vessel over 50 metres (or possibly less) aground.

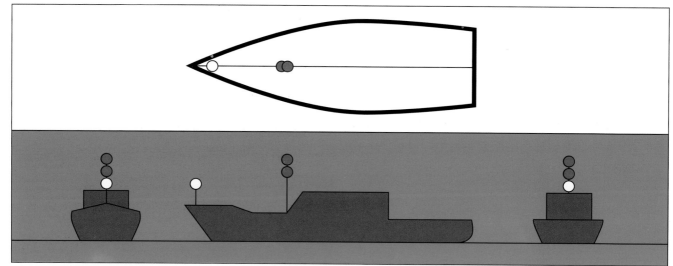

Figure 30.2 Lights for vessels aground.
  b. Vessel under 50 metres aground. (Compare with lights for a vessel not under command, making way, seen from astern).

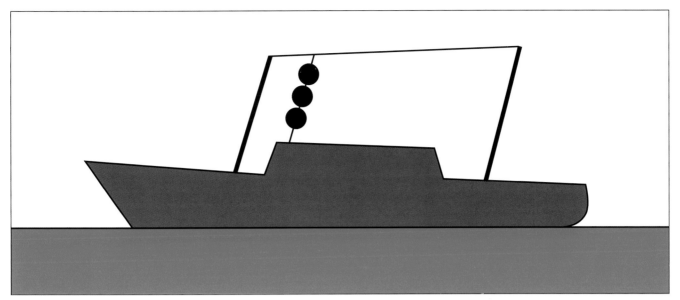

Figure 30.3 Day shape for vessel aground.

black ball) and not under command (two black balls) being displayed at the same time.

I have a friend who insists that three balls are shown for a vessel aground, because somebody has made a "balls up" of the navigation, but I doubt that the editor will let me write that!

> e.   A vessel of less than 7 metres in length, when at anchor, not in or near a narrow channel, fairway or anchorage, or where other vessels normally navigate, shall not be required to exhibit the lights or shape prescribed in paragraphs a. and b. of this Rule.

A small vessel less than 7 metres does not have to show any anchor light or shape, provided it is not anchored in or near a narrow channel, fairway or where other vessels might navigate.

> f.   A vessel of less than 12 metres in length, when aground, shall not be required to exhibit the lights or shapes prescribed in sub-paragraphs d. i. and ii. of this Rule.

A vessel of less than 12 metres does not have to show the signals for being aground, but it has to be able to show the signals for being at anchor. Every vessel over 12 metres is supposed to carry the three balls, and be able to show two all-round red lights, in addition to the anchor light.

Local rules may exist for special anchor signals or lights to be shown by inconspicuous objects or vessels, or there might be dispensation granted for vessels to show no lights at all, if anchored in a recognised anchorage. Such rules can usually be found in the pilot book for the area concerned.

Summary of Rule 30 – Anchored Vessels and Vessels Aground.

1. *At anchor, or on a mooring, all vessels over 7 metres should display a black ball in the forward part of the vessel by day.*
2. *At night, all vessels over 7 metres must show an all-round white light, where it can best be seen. Vessels over 50 metres must display two all-round white lights, one forward and a second one aft, with the after one at a lower level. Vessels over 100 metres must, and smaller vessels may use their decklights to make them more conspicuous when at anchor.*
3. *A vessel aground, by day shows three black balls in a vertical line – two balls for not under command and one for at anchor. (All three balls, because somebody made a "balls up" of the navigation!)*
4. *By night, the signal for aground is the two all-round red lights of not under command and the all round white light or lights (must be two if the vessel is over 50 metres) for the anchor signal. (Remember two reds and a single white could be a vessel less than 50 metres aground, or a vessel not under command, making way, seen from astern).*
5. *Vessels under 12 metres are exempted from showing the signals for being aground.*

Rule 31. Seaplanes

> Where it is impracticable for a seaplane to exhibit lights and shapes of the characteristics or in the positions prescribed in the Rules of this part she shall exhibit lights and shapes as closely similar in characteristics and position as is possible.

A seaplane on the water, when underway, will show red and green sidelights from the wing tips and a white stern light from the tail, just as she will when she is flying. In addition, a seaplane will usually show a white "masthead" light from somewhere in the forward part of the aircraft, or a flashing white strobe light.

When anchored at night, a seaplane will show white lights fore and aft, and will probably also show a white light at each wing tip.

Remember Rule 18 tasks a seaplane with keeping clear of all other vessels, and avoiding impeding their passage, but if there is a risk of collision, the seaplane is expected to comply with the normal steering Rules.

Summary of Rule 31 – Seaplanes.

When on the water, a seaplane will, as far as possible, show the same lights as a power-driven vessel, both when underway and at anchor.

Part D.
SOUND AND LIGHT SIGNALS
(Rules 32–37)

Rule 32. Definitions

> a.   The word "whistle" means any sound signalling appliance capable of producing the prescribed blasts and which complies with the specifications in Annex III to these regulations.

Annex III gives three different frequency bands for whistles on vessels of various sizes. Generally speaking, it means that the bigger the vessel, the deeper must be the tone of the whistle.

It also gives a table with the audible range of whistles on various sized vessels.

Length of vessel	Audible range required
200 metres or more:	2 nautical miles
200 to 75 metres:	1.5 miles
20 to 75 metres:	1 mile
Less than 20 metres:	0.5 mile

It then stresses that this table is for information only, and it warns that the range at which a signal might be heard is very dependent on the conditions.

The whistle or whistles must be positioned as high as possible, not only to reduce the chance of the sound being blocked by obstructions, but also to reduce the risk of damaging the hearing of people on board the vessel.

> b.   The term "short blast" means a blast of about one second's duration.
>
> c.   The term "prolonged blast" means a blast of from four to six seconds' duration.

All whistle signals stipulated in the Rules are defined in terms of short blasts (one second) and prolonged blasts (four to six seconds).

Summary of Rule32 – Definitions.

1. *The specifications for sound signal apparatus are given in Annex III. The audible ranges are:*

Length of vessel	*Audible range required*
200 metres or more:	*2 nautical miles*
200 to 75 metres:	*1.5 miles*
20 to 75 metres:	*1 mile*
Less than 20 metres:	*0.5 mile*

2. *A short blast is one second and a prolonged blast is four to six seconds.*

Rule 33. Equipment for Sound Signals

> a.   A vessel of 12 metres or more in length shall be provided with a whistle and a bell and a vessel of 100 metres or more in length shall, in addition, be provided with a gong, the tone and sound of which cannot be confused with that of the bell. The whistle, bell and gong shall comply with the specifications in Annex III to these regulations. The bell or gong or both may be replaced by other equipment having the same respective sound characteristics, provided that manual sounding of the prescribed signals shall always be possible.

Every vessel over 12 metres has to have a whistle and a bell. The whistle is for sounding fog signals and manoeuvring signals, and we shall see that the bell is required for giving signals when at anchor or aground in restricted visibility.

Vessels 100 metres or more in length have to carry a gong, the noise of which cannot be confused with the bell. Vessels over 100 metres in length must sound the gong in the after part of the vessel when anchored, or aground in restricted visibility.

Annex III gives specifications for the construction and size of the bell and the gong.

The Rule allows for the bell and/or the gong to be replaced by other equipment which sounds the same, so automatic or electronic equipment is allowed, but it must also be possible to sound the equipment manually, using alternative equipment if necessary.

> b.   A vessel of less than 12 metres in length shall not be obliged to carry the sound signalling appliances prescribed in paragraph a. of this Rule but if she does not, she shall be provided with some other means of making an efficient sound signal.

Vessels less than 12 metres do not have to carry the stipulated sound signalling apparatus, but if they don't carry it, then they must have some alternative means of making a suitable sound signal.

A portable compressed gas foghorn would probably be deemed to be adequate to replace the whistle, although the gas canisters do not have sufficient capacity for prolonged use.

Rule 34. Manoeuvring and Warning Signals

> a. When vessels are in sight of one another, a power-driven vessel underway, when manoeuvring as authorised or required by these Rules, shall indicate that manoeuvre by the following signals on her whistle:
>
> - one short blast to mean "I am altering my course to starboard";
> - two short blasts to mean "I am altering my course to port";
> - three short blasts to mean "I am operating astern propulsion".

Power-driven vessels shall give the manoeuvring signals when they are manoeuvring in accordance with the Rules, and they are in sight of another vessel. It is not discretionary – the Rule says the signals shall be given.

Sailing vessels are not obliged to give the signals when manoeuvring, but may do so if they choose.

If another vessel has been detected by radar, but cannot be sighted visually, then the signals should not be given. The vessels must be in visual sight of each other. However, a vessel would not be excused from giving the signals just because the other vessel had not been sighted because of a poor look-out being kept.

The signals are:
- One short blast – I am altering to starboard
- Two short blasts – I am altering to port
- Three short blasts – I am operating astern propulsion.

The term "operating astern propulsion" has been used to include those vessels which go astern by changing the pitch of the propeller, as well as those which use a gearbox, or change the direction of rotation of the engines. The three blasts does not indicate that the vessel is moving astern – it only indicates that it is "operating astern propulsion".

The signals would not have to be given for helm alterations that are applied to correct for the effects of wind or tide, but if even a small alteration of course is made, which is required by the Rules, to prevent a collision situation arising, then the correct signal must be given.

If another vessel is sighted at a long range, and an alteration of course is made before a risk of collision is deemed to exist, then the signals do not have to be given. However, as soon as there is a risk of collision, and a vessel makes an alteration of course, then the correct sound signal must be made, even if the distance between the vessels makes it unlikely that the other vessel will hear the signal. If the other vessel is in sight (no mention of hearing!), and there is a risk of collision, then the signals must be given.

> b. Any vessel may supplement the whistle signals prescribed in paragraph a. of this Rule by light signals, repeated as appropriate, whilst the manoeuvre is being carried out:
>
> i. these light signals shall have the following significance:
> - one flash to mean "I am altering my course to starboard";
> - two flashes to mean "I am altering my course to port";
> - three flashes to mean "I am operating astern propulsion".
>
> ii. the duration of each flash shall be about one second, the interval between flashes shall be about one second, and the interval between successive signals shall be not less than ten seconds;
>
> iii. the light used for this signal shall, if fitted, be an all-round white light, visible at a minimum range of 5 miles, and shall comply with the provisions of Annex I to these regulations.

This, and subsequent paragraphs refer to any vessel – power-driven or sailing vessels. A vessel may supplement the sound signals with a light signal, but there is no obligation to do so.

Annex I, Section 12 states that the manoeuvring light should be fitted in the same fore and aft vertical plane as the masthead light or lights. If only one masthead light is fitted, then the manoeuvring light should be carried where it can best be seen, but it must be at least 2 metres above or below the masthead light. If there are two masthead lights, then, if practicable, the manoeuvring light should be carried at least 2 metres above the forward masthead light, but it must be not less than 2 metres above or below the after masthead light.

The operation of the manoeuvring light does not have to be synchronised with the sound signal, and whereas the sound signal is generally only given once, the light signal can, and should, be repeated, with a gap of ten seconds between successive signals. A repeated flashing light signal could well be more conspicuous over a longer range than the sound signal, particularly at night.

The light signals are the same as the sound signals, namely:
- One flash – I am altering my course to starboard.
- Two flashes – I am altering my course to port.
- Three flashes – I am operating astern propulsion.

---

c. When in sight of one another in a narrow channel or fairway:

i. a vessel intending to overtake another shall in compliance with Rule 9e. indicate her intention by the following signals on her whistle:
- two prolonged blasts followed by one short blast to mean "I intend to overtake you on your starboard side";
- two prolonged blasts followed by two short blasts to mean "I intend to overtake you on your port side".

ii. the vessel about to be overtaken when acting in accordance with Rule 9e. shall indicate her agreement by the following signal on her whistle:
- one prolonged, one short, one prolonged and one short blast in that order.

Remember that the vessels must be in sight of one another for this Rule to apply. If the other vessel has been detected only by radar, then no manoeuvring signals are given, just the fog signals of **Rule 35**.

Rule 9 – Narrow Channels, told us in **Section e**. that if a vessel is overtaking another in a narrow channel or fairway, and the vessel which is to be overtaken has to take action to permit safe passing, then the overtaking vessel shall sound the appropriate signal. This part of **Rule 34** specifies those signals:

- Two prolonged and a short blast – I intend to overtake on your starboard side.
- Two prolonged and two short blasts – I intend to overtake on your port side.

If the vessel to be overtaken is in agreement, she shall sound the signal for agreement:

- Prolonged, short, prolonged, short blasts.

This is Morse code for the letter "C", and the International Code Flag "C" means "Affirmative". (Remember "C" sounds like the Spanish "Si", which means "Yes".)

Even after the vessel which is to be overtaken has sounded her agreement, the overtaking vessel is still obliged to keep out of her way. **Rule 13** – Overtaking, applies at all times, and an overtaking vessel is always obliged to keep out of the way of the overtaken vessel.

If the vessel which is to be overtaken does not agree with the overtaking vessel's request, or does not understand his intentions, then it can use the signal indicated in the next paragraph – at least five short and rapid blasts.

---

d. When vessels in sight of one another are approaching each other and from any cause either vessel fails to understand the intentions or actions of the other, or is in doubt whether sufficient action is being taken by the other to avoid collision, the vessel in doubt shall immediately indicate such doubt by giving at least five short and rapid blasts on the whistle. Such signal may be supplemented by a light signal of at least five short and rapid flashes.

The signal of at least five short and rapid blasts, which may be supplemented with a light signal of at least five short and rapid flashes, is often called the wake-up signal. As we saw in the previous paragraph, it can be used by a vessel which does not agree with, or does not understand the intentions of a vessel trying to overtake.

The wake-up signal should also be used by any vessel, whenever the intentions of another vessel, which is in sight, are not understood, or if it appears that they are not taking the action, or sufficient action, which is required by any of the Rules.

Rule 16 says that the Give-way vessel must take early and substantial action to keep well clear. **Rule 17** says that the Stand-on vessel is allowed to take action as soon as it becomes apparent that the give-way vessel is not taking appropriate action. The Stand-on vessel should sound the "Wake-up" signal, then sound the appropriate manoeuvring signal as she alters course (one blast – altering to starboard, two blasts – altering to port, which is generally to be avoided!). If she engages astern propulsion, then she should sound three blasts.

The wake-up signal can be repeated as often as necessary to attract the attention of the other vessel.

The Rule says that the sound signal can be supplemented with a light signal. There is no obligation to use the all-round white manoeuvring light, if fitted. A signal lamp could be used to send a brighter beam of light at the vessel in question, to attract their attention.

> e.   A vessel nearing a bend or an area of a channel or fairway where other vessels may be obscured by an intervening obstruction shall sound one prolonged blast. Such signal shall be answered with a prolonged blast by any approaching vessel that may be within hearing around the bend or behind the intervening obstruction.

A vessel which is approaching a blind bend, where other vessels may be obscured from sight, shall sound a prolonged blast. It is not a matter for discretion. If there is a chance that other vessels could be obscured, then the signal must be sounded.

Any vessel hearing the signal from around a bend or behind an obstruction shall answer with a prolonged blast.

> f.   If whistles are fitted on a vessel at a distance apart of more than 100 metres, one whistle only shall be used for giving manoeuvring and warning signals.

Annex III states that if two whistles are fitted, and they are more than 100 metres apart, then they must not be sounded simultaneously. That point is amplified in this part of the Rule. If two whistles were used, and they were more than 100 metres apart, other vessels might think that there were two vessels approaching.

Many Coastal States have additional rules for sound signals. A common one is that vessels must sound a prolonged blast before leaving their berth. Local rules may also stipulate the use of a VHF radio to confirm overtaking manoeuvres. In many areas it is common to hear one vessel telling another by VHF that they will "pass on one whistle". This means that the vessel intends to overtake the other on her starboard side.

Summary of Rule 34 – Manoeuvring and warning signals.

1. *When two vessels are in sight of one another, and one is manoeuvring as authorised or required by the Rules, a power-driven vessel shall, and a sailing vessel may sound the manoeuvring signals:*
   - *One short blast – I am altering course to starboard*
   - *Two short blasts – I am altering course to port*
   - *Three short blasts – I am operating astern propulsion (it does not mean that the vessel is making way astern, merely that she is operating astern propulsion.)*

   These sound signals may be supplemented with a light signal, using one, two or three flashes of one second duration. The light signal may be repeated at 10 second intervals.

2. *If a vessel wishes to overtake another vessel in a narrow channel or fairway, and the vessel to be overtaken has to take action to facilitate passing, then the overtaking vessel shall sound:*
   - *Two prolonged and a short blast – I intend to overtake on your starboard side.*
   - *Two prolonged and two short blasts – I intend to overtake on your port side.*

   If the vessel to be overtaken agrees, she shall sound Morse "C" – prolonged, short, prolonged and short blasts. If she disagrees, she shall sound at least five short and rapid blasts – the Wake-up signal.

3. *The Wake-up signal of at least five short and rapid blasts shall be sounded by any vessel which does not understand the intentions of another vessel that is in sight, or if another vessel does not appear to be taking the correct or sufficient action to avoid a collision as required by these Rules.*

4. *A vessel approaching a bend or obstruction in a narrow channel, which could obscure other vessels, shall sound a prolonged blast. Any vessel approaching the bend or obstruction which hears this signal, shall reply with a prolonged blast.*

5. *If a vessel has two whistles, and they are more than 100 metres apart, then only one is to be used for the manoeuvring or warning signals.*

Rule 35. Sound Signals in Restricted visibility

Rule 19 – Restricted visibility – applies in or near areas of restricted visibility, so a vessel navigating close to a fog bank, for example, even if it itself is in good visibility, is expected not only to comply with **Rule 19**, but also to sound the appropriate fog signal stipulated in **Rule 35**.

What constitutes restricted visibility for the purposes of this Rule is not easy to define. There is probably little reason to sound the fog signal if the visibility exceeds the range over which it is likely that the fog signal could be heard.

Annex III gives the expected range of audibility of sound signal appliances for various vessels. These are:
- Vessels over 200 metres — 2 miles
- 75 to 200 metres — 1.5 miles
- 20 to 75 metres — 1 mile
- Under 20 metres — 0.5 miles

Although there is a possibility of sound signals being heard at greater or lesser distances, these ranges give an indication of what various vessels might consider to be restricted visibility, and when they should sound their fog signals.

However, **Rule 19** could be applicable over greater distances. **Rule 19** applies whenever vessels are not in sight of one another, when in or near areas of restricted visibility, with particular emphasis being placed on vessels which are detected by radar, but are not in sight of each other. For example, a small vessel, under 20 metres, which detects another vessel by radar at a distance of say 5 miles, in 2 mile visibility, should expect to be bound by **Rule 19**. The small vessel should begin to plot the target, and if there is the possibility of a close-quarters situation developing, it should initiate a suitable manoeuvre, but there would be no point in sounding its fog signal, while the visibility remained at 2 miles, since there is little likelihood of the signal being heard from much over half a mile away.

Notice that **Rule 35** starts by telling us that the stipulated fog signals must be made by day and by night, if the vessel is in <u>or near</u> restricted visibility.

> In or near an area of restricted visibility, whether by day or by night, the signals prescribed in this Rule shall be used as follows:
> a.   A power-driven vessel making way through the water shall sound at intervals of not more than 2 minutes one prolonged blast.

All the sound signals for vessels underway are given at intervals of **not more than 2 minutes**. If it is known that there is another vessel in the vicinity, then the signals should be given more often, to assist the other vessel, which may not have radar, in determining the bearing of your vessel. Remember that a prolonged blast is 4 to 6 seconds – **Rule 32**.

A power-driven vessel <u>making way</u> through the water, sounds a prolonged blast every two minutes or less.

> b.   A power-driven vessel underway, but stopped and making no way through the water shall sound at intervals of not more than 2 minutes two prolonged blasts in succession with an interval of about 2 seconds between them.

A power-driven vessel which is underway, but stopped in the water, sounds two prolonged blasts (4 to 6 seconds each) every two minutes or less. The signal is sounded when a vessel is stopped in the water. The signal is not to be given when the engines are stopped, but only when the vessel actually comes to a complete stop in the water. The International Code Flag "M" also signifies that the "vessel is stopped in the water and is making no way", and the Morse Code for "M" is two dashes – i.e. two prolonged blasts.

> c.   A vessel not under command, a vessel restricted in her ability to manoeuvre, a vessel constrained by her draught, a sailing vessel, a vessel engaged in fishing and a vessel engaged in towing or pushing another vessel shall, instead of the signals prescribed

> in paragraphs a. or b. of this Rule, sound at intervals of not more than 2 minutes three blasts in succession, namely one prolonged followed by two short blasts.

All hampered or privileged vessels sound the same signal. Once again it is given at intervals of **not more than two minutes**, and the signal is a prolonged (4 to 6 seconds) followed by two short blasts (about one second each). Unlike power-driven vessels, these vessels sound the same signal any time they are underway, even if they are stopped in the water.

Vessels should sound this signal in the following circumstances:

- Not under command
- Restricted in ability to manoeuvre
- Constrained by draught
- Sailing vessel
- Vessel engaged in fishing
- Vessel engaged in towing or pushing

As we shall see in the next paragraph, vessels fishing at anchor, or vessels restricted in their ability to manoeuvre which are working at anchor sound this same signal of a prolonged and two short blasts. All other vessels in this list, when at anchor, would sound the normal signals for being at anchor, as indicated in **paragraph g**.

When International Code Flag "D" is flown, it requests other vessels to "Keep clear of me, I am manoeuvring with difficulty". "D" in Morse Code is a dash and two dots – i.e. a prolonged and two short blasts.

> d.   A vessel engaged in fishing, when at anchor, and a vessel restricted in her ability to manoeuvre when carrying out her work at anchor, shall instead of the signals prescribed in paragraph g. (signals when at anchor) of this Rule sound the signal prescribed in paragraph c.(prolonged and two short blasts) of the Rule.

Vessels when engaged in fishing while they are at anchor, not only continue to show the shapes and lights for fishing vessels – **Rule 26**, but also, in restricted visibility, they sound the signal of a hampered vessel (one prolonged and two short blasts) rather than the signal for a vessel at anchor. If, however, a fishing vessel is at anchor, but is not actually fishing, then it sounds the normal signals for a vessel at anchor.

Similarly, a vessel which is restricted in her ability to manoeuvre, but is operating at anchor, continues to show the lights and shapes of a vessel restricted in her ability to manoeuvre. In restricted visibility, she sounds the signal of a hampered vessel (one prolonged and two short blasts) rather than the signals for a vessel at anchor.

> e. A vessel towed or if more than one vessel is towed the last vessel of the tow, if manned, shall at intervals of not more than 2 minutes sound four blasts in succession, namely one prolonged followed by three short blasts. When practicable, this signal shall be made immediately after the signal made by the towing vessel.

There is only an obligation to sound a fog signal from the towed vessel if it is manned. There is no obligation to do so if it is not manned. However, under such circumstances it would be prudent to ensure that the towed vessel was manned, as it is not possible for other vessels to determine that the vessel is a tug with a tow by its signal of one prolonged and two short blasts.

The tow sounds its signal of a prolonged and three short blasts immediately after the tug has sounded its own signal of a prolonged and two short blasts, which must be made every two minutes or less.

In Morse Code, a dash and three dots (prolonged and three short blasts) signifies the letter "B". The International Code flag "B" indicates that the vessel is carrying (or loading) a dangerous cargo. I suppose a towed barge, particularly on a dark and foggy night, could possibly be considered as a dangerous cargo!

> f. When a pushing vessel and a vessel being pushed ahead are rigidly connected in a composite unit they shall be regarded as a power-driven vessel and shall give the signals prescribed in paragraphs a. or b. of this Rule.

We saw under **Rule 24 –** Towing and Pushing, that when a pushing vessel and a vessel being pushed are rigidly connected in a composite unit, they do not show the lights nor shapes for a towing vessel – they are simply lit as a power-driven vessel. Similarly, in restricted visibility, they do not sound any special signals – only those for a power-driven vessel – one prolonged blast every two minutes or less if making way, or two prolonged blasts every two minutes or less if stopped in the water.

> g. A vessel at anchor shall at intervals of not more than one minute ring the bell rapidly for about 5 seconds. In a vessel of 100 metres or more in length the bell shall be sounded in the forepart of the vessel and immediately after the ringing of the bell the gong shall be sounded rapidly for about 5 seconds in the after part of the vessel. A vessel at anchor may in addition sound three blasts in succession, namely one short, one prolonged and one short blast, to give warning of her position and of the possibility of collision to an approaching vessel.

We have seen that vessels underway (whether they are making way or stopped in the water) give the appropriate signals at least every two minutes. Now we see that vessels at anchor must give the signals at least _every minute_.

The basic fog signal for a vessel at anchor is a bell rung rapidly for five seconds, and as we have just seen, this must be done at least every minute.

If the vessel is 100 metres or more in length, then the bell must be rung in the forward part of the vessel, and a gong in the after part. Both are sounded for five seconds, with the gong being sounded immediately after the bell.

Because the distance that the bell and/or the gong is likely to be heard is quite short, provision is made for vessels at anchor to sound their whistle to warn other vessels of their location. This signal is a short, a prolonged and a short blast – this is Morse Code for "R". (In the International Code of Signals, "R" is the only flag which is not allocated a meaning.)

> h. A vessel aground shall give the bell signal and if required the gong signal prescribed in paragraph g. of this Rule and shall, in addition, give three separate and distinct strokes on the bell immediately before and after the rapid ringing of the bell. A vessel aground may in addition sound an appropriate whistle signal.

A vessel aground gives the bell signal, and if she is 100 metres or more the gong signal, but immediately before, and immediately after the ringing of the bell, three distinct strokes are made on the bell. So the signal for a vessel under 100 metres aground is 3 strokes on the bell, 5 seconds of rapid ringing, and 3 strokes on the bell, repeated at least every minute. For a vessel 100 metres or more aground, the signal is 3 strokes, 5 seconds of rapid ringing, 3 strokes on the bell, followed immediately by 5 seconds rapid sounding of the gong aft, repeated at least every minute.

The Rule states that a vessel aground, in addition to the stipulated signals, _may_ **sound an appropriate whistle signal.** No signal is stipulated, because the delegates at the conference could not agree on a suitable signal that would be appropriate in all circumstances. International Code Flag "U" says "You are standing into danger". "U" in Morse Code is 2 dots and a dash, so 2 short and one prolonged blast on the whistle would generally be the most appropriate signal to warn other vessels of the danger. "U" is also a fog signal which is often chosen to be sounded from offshore oil installations, and similar fixed structures.

> i. A vessel of less than 12 metres in length shall not be obliged to give the above-mentioned signals but, if she does not, shall make some other efficient sound signal at intervals of not more than 2 minutes.

Rule 33 exempted small vessels, under 12 metres, from complying with the requirements to carry "proper" sound signalling apparatus, only requiring them to be able to make some kind of efficient sound signal. This paragraph is continuing the exemption, and requires vessels under 12 metres to make "an efficient sound signal" at least every two minutes. It does not stipulate whether the vessel is underway or at anchor, so presumably a small vessel is entitled to make her signal every 2 minutes when at anchor as well as when underway.

As we noted in **Rule 33**, a portable foghorn with a canister of compressed gas would probably be classed as making a suitable sound signal, but remember that each canister can only sound a finite number of blasts.

> j.   A pilot vessel when engaged on pilotage duty may in addition to the signals prescribed in paragraphs a., b., or g. of this Rule sound an identity signal consisting of four short blasts.

A pilot vessel is obliged to sound the signals of a normal vessel, whether it is making way (one prolonged blast at least every 2 minutes), stopped in the water (2 prolonged blasts at least every 2 minutes) or at anchor (5 seconds on the bell at least every minute, with an additional 5 seconds on the gong in the unlikely event that the pilot vessel is 100 metres or more in length). Although the Rule does not state it, presumably if the pilot vessel were operating under sail, then she would sound a prolonged and two short blasts, as any other sailing vessel would.

In addition, a pilot vessel on duty _may_ sound four short blasts on the whistle. In Morse Code 4 dots is "H", and International Code Flag "H" signifies that the vessel has a pilot on board. The 4 short blasts are to be sounded in addition to the other signals, and will generally follow the sounding of the other signal.

Summary of Rule 35 – Sound Signals in Restricted Visibility.

1. _Vessels operating in or near areas of restricted visibility must make the appropriate sound signals by day or by night._
2. _When under way, the sound signals are made at least every 2 minutes, and when at anchor, at least every minute._
3. _A power-driven vessel underway and making way sounds one prolonged blast (4 to 6 seconds) at least every 2 minutes._
4. _A power-driven vessel underway but stopped in the water sounds "M" – 2 prolonged blasts at least every 2 minutes._
5. _Vessels not under command, restricted in ability to manoeuvre, constrained by draught, sailing vessels, vessels fishing and towing or pushing another vessel all_

sound "D" – one prolonged and 2 short blasts at least every 2 minutes when they are underway, even if they are stopped in the water._
6. _Vessels fishing at anchor, or vessels restricted in their ability to manoeuvre working at anchor continue to sound "D" while at anchor – all other vessels sound the normal anchor signals which are 5 seconds rapid ringing of the bell at least every minute, and if the vessel is 100 metres or more, this is followed by 5 seconds rapid sounding of the gong in the after part of the vessel. Vessels at anchor may in addition sound "R" on the whistle – one short, one prolonged and one short blast on the whistle to warn other vessels._
7. _Vessels being towed, if they are manned, sound one prolonged and 3 short blasts, immediately after the tug has sounded her one prolonged and 2 short blasts._
8. _Vessels aground sound 3 strokes on the bell, followed by 5 seconds of rapid ringing, followed by a further 3 strokes. If they are 100 metres or more in length, this signal is followed by 5 seconds of rapid sounding of the gong aft._
9. _A vessel aground may sound an appropriate signal on the whistle – this would generally be "U" – You are standing into danger – 2 short blasts followed by one prolonged blast._
10. _Vessels under 12 metres are only required to make "an efficient sound signal" every 2 minutes._
11. _Pilot vessels, when on duty, may sound "H" – 4 short blasts on the whistle, in addition to the signals of a vessel making way, stopped in the water or at anchor, as appropriate._

Rule 36.   Signals to Attract Attention

> If necessary to attract the attention of another vessel any vessel may make light or sound signals that cannot be mistaken for any signal authorised elsewhere in these Rules, or may direct the beam of her searchlight in the direction of the danger, in such a way as not to embarrass any vessel. Any light to attract the attention of another vessel shall be such that it cannot be mistaken for any aid to navigation. For the purpose of this Rule the use of high intensity intermittent or revolving lights, such as strobe lights, shall be avoided.

When a vessel wishes to attract the attention of another, it must not use signals which may be confused with signals authorised in the Rules for identifying a particular type of vessel, signals indicating manoeuvres, or signals indicating distress.

It is suggested that a searchlight can be used to indicate danger, but warns against "embarrassing" the other vessel – this means that you should not shine the light into the eyes of helmsman or lookout on the other vessel.

If the whistle is used, the "wake-up" signal of at least 5 short and rapid blasts would be better than one extremely long blast, which could be miss-interpreted as the continuous sounding of the foghorn, which is one of the recognised distress signals.

The use of strobe lights is specifically prohibited, as they could easily be confused with the flashing light of a navigation buoy.

Other signals which might be used to attract attention include a white flare, shining a searchlight on the sails of a sailing vessel, or turning on the deck lights, provided that they do not interfere with the vision of the lookout or helmsman, nor mask the navigation lights or identifying lights of the vessel.

Summary of Rule 36 – Signals to attract attention.

1. *Vessels may make light or sound signals to attract the attention of another vessel, but they must be such that they cannot be confused with signals authorised in the Rules, including distress signals, nor be confused with lights for aids to navigation, such as buoys.*

Rule 37. Distress Signals

When a vessel is in distress and requires assistance she shall use or exhibit the signals described in Annex IV to these Regulations.

Annex IV states that any of the following signals can be displayed, separately, or several of them together, to indicate distress.

a. a gun or other explosive signal fired at intervals of about a minute;
b. a continuous sounding with any fog-signalling apparatus;
c. rockets or shell, throwing red stars fired one at a time at short intervals;
d. a signal made by radiotelephony or by any other signalling method consisting of the group ···－－－··· (SOS) in Morse Code;
e. a signal sent by radiotelephony consisting of the spoken word "Mayday";
f. the International Code Signal of distress indicated by N.C.;
g. a signal consisting of a square flag having above or below it a ball or anything resembling a ball;
h. flames on the vessel (as from burning tar barrel, oil barrel, etc.);
i. a rocket parachute flare or a hand flare showing a red light;

j. a smoke signal giving off orange-coloured smoke;
k. slowly and repeatedly raising and lowering arms outstretched to each side;
l. the radiotelegraph alarm signal;
m. the radiotelephone alarm signal;
n. signals transmitted by emergency position-indicating radio beacons;
o. approved signals transmitted by radiocommunication systems, including survival craft radar transponders.

2. The use or exhibition of any of the foregoing signals except for the purpose of indicating distress and need of assistance and the use of other signals which may be confused with any of the above signals is prohibited.

3. Attention is drawn to the relevant sections of the International Code of Signals, the Merchant Ship Search and Rescue Manual and the following signals:

a. a piece of orange-coloured canvas with either a black square and circle or other appropriate symbol (for identification from the air);
b. a dye marker.

The two signals from MERSAR, the Merchant Shipping Search and Rescue Manual – the orange flag with the black square and circle, and a dye marker, are additional to the "official" list. Why these two signals are not included in that list is just one of the little bureaucratic mysteries sent to try us!

Since this list was compiled, the Global Maritime Distress and Safety System (GMDSS) for marine communications has come into being. A Digital Selective Calling (DSC) Alert is now a recognised method of indicating distress, by VHF, MF and HF radio, as is a Distress Alert sent by Inmarsat A or C satellite systems. No doubt these will be included in future amendments.

Summary of Rule 37 – Distress Signals.

I found that the list of signals was easier to learn if they were arranged in a more logical order. The 15 stipulated distress signals from Annex IV are:

The six "electronic" signals:
1. *EPIRB.*
2. *SART.*
3. *Radiotelephony alarm – two tone signal on 2182 MHz.*
4. *"Mayday" on the radio telephone.*
5. *Radio telegraphy alarm – tone on 500 MHz.*
6. *SOS (···－－－···) by telegraphy (or by any other means).*

Then the four "pyrotechnics":
1. *Red star shells or rockets.*
2. *Red parachute or hand flare.*
3. *Orange smoke signal.*
4. *Flames.*

Finally the two "noise" signals:
1. *Explosion every minute.*
2. *Continuous sounding of fog signal.*

The two signals from MERSAR, the Merchant Shipping Search and Rescue Manual are:
An orange flag with the black square and circle.
A dye marker.

The three "visual" signals:
1. *Code flags N and C.*
2. *Square flag and a round ball.*
3. *Raising and lowering arms.*

Under GMDSS, a DSC Alert can be used to indicate distress, by VHF, MF and HF radio, and a Distress Alert can be sent by Inmarsat A or C satellite systems. Although not included in the current Colregs, no doubt they will be soon.

Part E.
EXEMPTIONS

Rule 38. **Exemptions**

Any vessel (or class of vessels) provided that she complies with the requirements of the International Regulations for Preventing Collisions at Sea, 1960, the keel of which is laid or which is at a corresponding stage of construction before the entry into force of these Regulations, may be exempted from compliance therewith as follows:

a. The installation of lights with ranges prescribed in Rule 22, until four years after the date of entry into force of these Regulations.

b. The installation of lights with colour specifications as prescribed in Section 7 of Annex I to these Regulations, until four years after the date of entry into force of these Regulations.

c. The repositioning of lights as a result of conversion from Imperial to metric units and rounding off measurement figures, permanent exemption.

d. i. The repositioning of masthead lights on vessels of less than 150 metres in length, resulting from the prescriptions of Section 3.a. of Annex I to these Regulations, permanent exemption.
ii. The repositioning of masthead lights on vessels of 150 metres or more in length, resulting from the prescriptions of Section 3.a. of Annex I to these Regulations, until nine years after the date of entry into force of these Regulations.

e. The repositioning of masthead lights resulting from the prescriptions of Section 2.b. of Annex I to these Regulations, until nine years after the date of entry into force of these Regulations.

f. The repositioning of sidelights resulting from the prescriptions of Sections 2.g. and 3.b. of Annex I to these Regulations, until nine years after the date of entry into force of these Regulations.

g. The requirements for sound signal appliances prescribed in Annex III to these Regulations, until nine years after the date of entry into force of these Regulations.

h. The repositioning of all-round lights resulting from the prescription of Section 9.b. of Annex I to these Regulations, permanent exemption.

This Rule was included to allow time for existing vessels to comply with the Rules after various changes were introduced, and the requirement to re-position some lights when the measurements were changed from Imperial to metric.

Annex I.
POSITIONING AND TECHNICAL DETAILS OF LIGHTS AND SHAPES

Most salient points have been included in the text for the various Rules. The Annex is included here in its entirety for completeness.

1. *Definition.*
The term "height above the hull" means the height above the uppermost continuous deck. This height shall be measured from the position vertically beneath the location of the light.

2. *Vertical positioning and spacing of lights.*

a. On a power-driven vessel of 20 metres or more in length the masthead lights shall be placed as follows:

i. the forward masthead light, or if only one masthead light is carried, then that light, at a height above the hull of not less than 6 metres, and, if the breadth of the hull exceeds 6 metres, then at a height above the hull of not less than such breadth, so however that the light need not be placed at a greater height above the hull than 12 metres;

ii. when two masthead lights are carried the after one shall be at least 4.5 metres vertically higher than the forward one.

b. The vertical separation of the masthead lights of power-driven vessels shall be such that in all normal conditions of trim the after light will be seen over and separate from the forward light at a distance of 1,000 metres from the stem when viewed from sea level.

c. The masthead light of a power-driven vessel of 12 metres but less than 20 metres in length shall be placed at a height of not less than 2.5 metres.

d. A power-driven vessel of less than 12 metres in length may carry the uppermost light at a height of less than 2.5 metres above the gunwale. When however a masthead light is carried in addition to sidelights and a sternlight or the all-round light prescribed in Rule 23 c.i. is carried in addition to sidelights, then such masthead light shall be carried at least 1 metre higher than the sidelights.

e. One of the two or three masthead lights prescribed for a power-driven vessel when engaged in towing or pushing another vessel shall be placed in the same position as either the forward masthead light or the after masthead light; provided that, if carried on the aftermast, the lowest after masthead light shall be at least 4.5 metres vertically higher that the forward masthead light.

f. i. The masthead light or lights prescribed in Rule 23 a. shall be so placed as to be above and clear of all other lights and obstructions except as described in sub-paragraph ii.

ii. When it is impracticable to carry the all-round lights prescribed by Rule 27 b.i. or Rule 28 below the masthead lights, they may be carried above the after masthead light(s) or vertically in between the forward masthead light(s) and after masthead light(s), provided that in the latter case the requirement of Section 3 c. of this Annex shall be complied with.

g. The sidelights of a power-driven vessel shall be placed at a height above the hull not greater than three-quarters of that of the forward masthead light. They shall not be so low as to be interfered with by deck lights.

h. The sidelights, if in a combined lantern and carried on a power-driven vessel of less than 20 metres in length, shall be placed not less than 1 metre below the masthead light.

i. When the Rules prescribe two or three lights to be carried in a vertical line, they shall be spaced as follows:

i. on a vessel of 20 metres in length or more such lights shall be spaced not less than 2 metres apart, and the lowest of these lights shall, except where a towing light is required, be placed at a height of not less than 4 metres above the hull;

ii. on a vessel of less than 20 metres in length such lights shall be spaced not less than 1 metre apart and the lowest of these lights shall, except where a towing light is required, be placed at a height of not less than 2 metres above the gunwale;

iii. when three lights are carried they shall be equally spaced.

j. The lower of the two all-round lights prescribed for a vessel when engaged in fishing shall be at a height above the sidelights not less than twice the distance between the two vertical lights.

k. The forward anchor light prescribed in Rule 30 a. i., when two are carried, shall be not less than 4.5 metres above the after one. On a vessel of 50 metres or more in length this forward anchor light shall be placed at a height of not less than 6 metres above the hull.

3. *Horizontal positioning and spacing of lights.*

a. When two masthead lights are prescribed for a power-driven vessel, the horizontal distance between them shall not be less than one half of the length of the vessel but need not be more than 100 metres. The forward light shall be placed not more than one quarter of the length of the vessel from the stem.

b. On a power-driven vessel of 20 metres of more in length the sidelights shall not be placed in front of the forward masthead lights. They shall be placed at or near the side of the vessel.

c. When the lights prescribed in Rule 27 b. i. or Rule 28 are placed vertically between the forward masthead light(s) and the after masthead light(s) these all-round lights shall be placed at a horizontal distance of not less than 2 metres from the fore and aft centreline of the vessel in the athwartship direction.

d. When only one masthead light is prescribed for a power-driven vessel, this light shall be exhibited forward of amidships; except that a vessel of less than 20 metres in length need not exhibit this light forward of amidships but shall exhibit it as far forward as practicable.

4. *Details of location of direction-indicating lights for fishing vessels, dredgers and vessels engaged in underwater operations.*

a. The light indicating the direction of the outlying gear from a vessel engaged in fishing as prescribed in Rule 26 c. ii. shall be placed at a horizontal distance of not less than 2 metres and not more than 6 metres away from the two all-round red and white lights. This light shall be placed not higher than the all-round white light prescribed in Rule 26 c. i. and not lower than the sidelights.

b. The lights and shapes on a vessel engaged in dredging or underwater operations to indicate the obstructed side and/or the side on which it is safe to pass, as prescribed in Rule 27 d. i. and ii., shall be placed at the maximum practical horizontal distance, but in no case less than 2 metres, from the lights or shapes prescribed in Rule 27 b. i. and ii. In no case shall the upper of these lights or shapes be at a greater height than the lower of the three lights or shapes prescribed in Rule 27 b. i. and ii.

5. *Screens for sidelights.*

The sidelights for vessels of 20 metres or more in length shall be fitted with inboard screens painted matt black, and meeting the requirements of Section 9 of this Annex. On vessels of less than 20 metres in length the sidelights, if necessary to meet the requirements of Section 9 of this Annex, shall be fitted with inboard matt black screens. With a combined lantern, using a single vertical filament and a very narrow division between the green and red sections, external screens need not be fitted.

6. *Shapes.*

a. Shapes shall be black and of the following sizes:
i. a ball shall have a diameter of not less than 0.6 metre;
ii. a cone shall have a base diameter of not less than 0.6 metre and a height equal to its diameter;
iii. a cylinder shall have a diameter of at least 0.6 metre diameter and a height of twice its diameter;
iv. a diamond shape shall consist of two cones as defined in ii. above having a common base.

b. The vertical distance between shapes shall be at least 1.5 metres.

c. In a vessel of less than 20 metres in length shapes of lesser dimensions but commensurate with the size of vessel may be used and the distance apart may be correspondingly reduced.

7. *Colour specification of lights.*

The chromaticity of all navigation lights shall conform to the following standards, which lie within the boundaries of the area of the diagram specified for each colour by the International Commission on Illumination (CIE).

The boundaries of the area for each colour are given by indicating the corner co-ordinates, which are as follows:

i.	White					
x	0.525	0.525	0.452	0.310	0.310	0.443
y	0.382	0.440	0.440	0.348	0.283	0.382

ii.	Green			
x	0.028	0.009	0.300	0.203
y	0.385	0.723	0.511	0.356

iii.	Red			
x	0.680	0.660	0.735	0.721
y	0.320	0.320	0.265	0.259

iv.	Yellow			
x	0.612	0.618	0.575	0.575
y	0.382	0.382	0.425	0.406

(This is determining the actual colour of the various lights. If you buy an "approved" navigation light, it will have been tested to conform with these specifications.)

8. *Intensity of lights.*

a. The minimum luminous intensity of lights shall be calculated by using the formula:

$$I = 3.43 \times 10^6 \times T \times D^2 \times K^{-D}$$

where I is luminous intensity in candelas under service conditions,

T is the threshold factor 2×10^{-7}.
D is the range of visibility (luminous range) of the light in nautical miles.
K is atmospheric transmissivity.

For prescribed lights the value of K shall be 0.8 corresponding to a meteorological visibility of approximately 13 miles.

b. A selection of figures derived from the formula is given in the following table:

Range of visibility (luminous range) of light in nautical miles	Luminous intensity of light in candelas for K = 0.8
D	I
1	0.9
2	4.3
3	12
4	27
5	52
6	94

Note: The maximum luminous intensity of navigation lights should be limited to avoid undue glare. This shall not be achieved by a variable control of the luminous intensity.

9. *Horizontal sectors.*

a.

i. In the forward direction, sidelights as fitted on the vessel shall show the minimum required intensities. The intensities shall decrease to reach practical cut-off between 1 degree and 3 degrees outside the prescribed sectors.

ii. For sternlights and masthead lights and at 22.5 degrees abaft the beam for sidelights, the minimum required intensities shall be maintained over the arc of the horizon up to 5 degrees within the limits of the sectors prescribed in Rule 21. From 5 degrees within the prescribed sectors the intensity may decrease by 50 per cent, up to the prescribed limits; it shall decrease steadily to reach practical cut-off at not more than 5 degrees outside the prescribed sectors.

b.

i. All-round lights shall be so located as not to be obscured by masts, topmasts or structures within angular sectors of more than 6 degrees, except anchor lights prescribed in Rule 30, which need not be placed at an impracticable height above the hull.

ii. If it is impracticable to comply with paragraph b. i. of this section by exhibiting only one all-round light, two all-round lights shall be used suitably positioned or screened so that they appear, as far as practicable, as one light at a distance of one mile.

10. *Vertical sectors.*

a. The vertical sectors of electric lights, as fitted, with the exception of lights on sailing vessels underway shall ensure that:

i. at least the required minimum intensity is maintained at all angels from 5 degrees above to 5 degrees below the horizontal;

ii. at least 60 percent of the required minimum intensity is maintained from 7.5 degrees above to 7.5 degrees below the horizontal.

b. In the case of sailing vessels underway the vertical sectors of electric lights as fitted shall ensure that:

i. at least the required minimum intensity is maintained at all angles from 5 degrees above to 5 degrees below the horizontal;

ii. at least 50 percent of the required minimum intensity is maintained from 25 degrees above to 25 degrees below the horizontal.

c. In the case of lights other than electric these specifications shall be met as closely as possible.

11. *Intensity of non-electric lights.*

Non-electric lights shall so far as practicable comply with the minimum intensities, as specified in the Table given in section 8 of this Annex.

12. *Manoeuvring light.*

Notwithstanding the provisions of paragraph 2 f. of this Annex the manoeuvring light described in Rule 34 b. shall be placed in the same fore and aft vertical plane as the masthead light or lights and, where practicable, at a minimum height of 2 metres vertically above or below the after masthead light. On a vessel where only one masthead light is carried the manoeuvring light, if fitted, shall be carried where it can best be seen, not less than 2 metres vertically apart from the masthead light.

13. *High speed craft.*

The masthead light of high speed craft with a length to breadth ratio of less than 3.0 may be placed at a height related to the breadth of the craft lower than that prescribed in paragraph 2 a. i. of this Annex, provided that the base angel of the isosceles triangles formed by the sidelights and masthead light, when seen in elevation, is not less than 27°.

14. *Approval.*

The construction of lights and shapes and the installation of lights on board the vessel shall be to the satisfaction of the appropriate authority of the State whose flag the vessel is entitled to fly.

ANNEX II.
ADDITIONAL SIGNALS FOR FISHING VESSELS FISHING IN CLOSE PROXIMITY

Again, the most important points have been covered in the text for the specific Rules, but the annex is included for reference.

1. *General.*
The lights mentioned herein shall, if exhibited in pursuance of Rule 26 d., be placed where they can best be seen. They shall be at least 0.9 metre apart but at a lower level than lights prescribed in Rule 26 b. i. and c. i. The lights shall be visible all round the horizon at a distance of at least 1 mile but at a lesser distance then the lights prescribed by these Rules for fishing vessels.

2. *Signals for trawlers.*
a. Vessels of 20 metres or more in length when engaged in trawling, whether using demersal or pelagic gear, shall exhibit:
i. when shooting their nets:
two white lights in a vertical line;
ii. when hauling their nets:
one white light over one red light in a vertical line;
iii. when a net has come fast on an obstruction:
two red lights in a vertical line.

b. Each vessel of 20 metres or more in length engaged in pair trawling shall exhibit:
i. by night, a searchlight directed forward and in the direction of the other vessel of the pair;
ii. when shooting or hauling their nets or when their nets have come fast upon an obstruction, the lights prescribed in 2 a. above.

c. A vessel of less than 20 metres in length engaged in trawling, whether using demersal or pelagic gear or engaged in pair trawling, may exhibit the lights prescribed in paragraphs a or b of this section, as appropriate.

3. *Signals for purse seiners.*
Vessels engaged in fishing with purse seine gear may exhibit two yellow lights in a vertical line. These lights shall flash alternately every second and with equal light and occultation duration. These lights may be exhibited only when the vessel is hampered by its fishing gear.

ANNEX III.
TECHNICAL DETAILS OF SOUND SIGNAL APPLIANCES

This annex covers the technical details of sound signal apparatus. We covered the effects of these requirements in the text for Rules 33 to 35.

1. *Whistles.*

a. *Frequencies and range of audibility.*

The fundamental frequency of the signal shall lie within the range 70-700 Hz. The range of audibility of the signal from a whistle shall be determined by those frequencies, which may include a fundamental and/or one or more higher frequencies, which lie within the range 180-700 Hz (+/- 1 per cent) and which provide the sound pressure levels specified in paragraph 1 c. below.

b. *Limits of fundamental frequencies.*

To ensure a wide variety of whistle characteristics, the fundamental frequency of a whistle shall be between the following limits:
  i. 70-200 Hz, for a vessel 200 metres or more in length;
  ii. 130-350 Hz, for a vessel 75 metres but less than 200 metres in length;
  iii. 250-700 Hz, for a vessel less than 75 metres in length.

c. *Sound signal intensity and range of audibility.*

A whistle fitted in a vessel shall provide, in the direction of maximum intensity of the whistle and at a distance of 1 metre from it, a sound pressure level in at least one 1/3rd-octave band within the range of frequencies 180-700 Hz (+/- 1 per cent) of not less than the appropriate figure given in the table below.

Length of vessel in metres	1/3rd-octave band level at 1 metre in dB referred to 2 x 10⁻⁵ N/m²	Audibility range in nautical miles
200 or more	143	2
75 but less than 200	138	1.5
20 but less than 75	130	1
Less than 20	120	0.5

The range of audibility in the table is for information and is approximately the range at which a whistle may be heard on its forward axis with 90 per cent probability in conditions of still air on board a vessel having average background noise level at the listening posts (taken to be 68 dB in the octave band centred on 250 Hz and 63 dB in the octave band centred on 500 Hz).

In practice the range at which a whistle may be heard is extremely variable and depends critically on weather conditions; the values given can be regarded as typical but under conditions of strong wind or high ambient noise level at the listening post the range may be much reduced.

d. *Directional properties.*

The sound pressure level of a directional whistle shall be not more than 4 dB below the prescribed sound pressure level on the axis at any direction in the horizontal plane within +/- 45 degrees of the axis. The sound pressure level at any other direction in the horizontal plane shall be not more than 10 dB below the prescribed sound pressure level on the axis, so that the range in any direction will be at least half the range on the forward axis. The sound pressure level shall be measured in that 1/3rd-octave band which determines the audibility range.

e. *Positioning of whistles.*

When a directional whistle is to be used as the only whistle signal on a vessel, it shall be installed with its maximum intensity directed straight ahead.

A whistle shall be placed as high as practicable on a vessel, in order to reduce interception of the emitted sound by obstructions and also to minimise hearing damage risk to personnel. The sound pressure level of the vessel's own signal at listening posts shall not exceed 110 dB (A) and so far as practicable should not exceed 100 dB (A).

f. *Fitting of more than one whistle.*

If whistles are fitted at a distance apart of more than

100 metres, it shall be so arranged that they are not sounded simultaneously.

g. *Combined whistle systems.*

If due to the presence of obstructions the sound field of a single whistle or of one of the whistles referred to in paragraph 1 f. above is likely to have a zone of greatly reduced signal level, it is recommended that a combined whistle system be fitted so as to overcome this reduction. For the purpose of the Rules a combined whistle system is to be regarded as a single whistle. The whistles of a combined system shall be located at a distance apart of not more than 100 metres and arranged to be sounded simultaneously. The frequency of any one whistle shall differ from those of the others by at least 10 Hz.

2. *Bell or gong.*
a. *Intensity of signal.*

A bell or gong, or other device having similar sound characteristics shall produce a sound pressure level of not less than 110 dB at a distance of 1 metre from it.

b. *Construction.*

Bells and gongs shall be made of corrosion-resistant material and designed to give a clear tone. The diameter of the mouth of the bell shall be not less than 300 mm. for vessels of 20 metres or more in length, and shall be not less than 200 mm. for vessels of 12 metres or more but of less than 20 metres in length. Where practicable, a power-driven striker is recommended to ensure constant force but manual operation shall be possible. The mass of the striker shall be not less than 3 per cent of the mass of the bell.

3. *Approval.*

The construction of sound signal appliances, their performance and their installation on board the vessel shall be to the satisfaction of the appropriate authority of the State whose flag the vessel is entitled to fly.

ANNEX IV.
DISTRESS SIGNALS

This is the annex which was quoted in Rule 37 – Distress Signals.

1. The following signals, used or exhibited either together or separately, indicate distress and need of assistance:

a. a gun or other explosive signal fired at intervals of about a minute;
b. a continuous sounding with any fog-signalling apparatus;
c. rockets or shells, throwing red stars fired one at a time at short intervals;
d. a signal made by radiotelephony or by any other signalling method consisting of the group ···−−−··· (SOS) in Morse Code;
e. a signal sent by radiotelephony consisting of the spoken word "Mayday";
f. the International Code Signal of distress indicated by N.C.;
g. a signal consisting of a square flag having above or below it a ball or anything resembling a ball;
h. flames on the vessel (as from burning tar barrel, oil barrel, etc.);
i. a rocket parachute flare or a hand flare showing a red light;
j. a smoke signal giving off orange-coloured smoke;
k. slowly and repeatedly raising and lowering arms outstretched to each side;
l. the radiotelegraph alarm signal;
m. the radiotelephone alarm signal;
n. signals transmitted by emergency position-indicating radio beacons;
o. approved signals transmitted by radiocommunication systems, including survival craft radar transponders.

2. The use or exhibition of any of the foregoing signals except for the purpose of indicating distress and need of assistance and the use of other signals which may be confused with any of the above signals is prohibited.

3. Attention is drawn to the relevant sections of the International Code of Signals, the Merchant Ship Search and Rescue Manual and the following signals:
a. a piece of orange-coloured canvas with either a black square and circle or other appropriate symbol (for identification from the air);
b. a dye marker.

USE OF RADAR
TO AVOID
COLLISIONS

Rule 5 tells us that every vessel shall at all times maintain a proper look-out by sight and hearing as well as by all available means appropriate in the prevailing circumstances and conditions so as to make a full appraisal of the situation and of the risk of collision. This means that if we have radar fitted to the vessel, then we must use it to make a full appraisal of the risk of collision.

Rule 7.a. tells us that every vessel shall use all available means appropriate to the prevailing circumstances and conditions to determine if risk of collision exists.

Just in case there is any doubt that this may or may not include the use of radar, Rule 7.b. spells it out for us – Proper use shall be made of radar equipment if fitted and operational, including long-range scanning to obtain early warning of risk of collision and radar plotting or equivalent systematic observation of detected objects.

So, we have been told that if we have radar, then not only must we use it to assess the risk of any collision, but we must do this by plotting or equivalent systematic observation of detected objects.

Rule 7.c. warns us that – Assumptions shall not be made on the basis of scanty information, especially scanty radar information. We should not alter course when we detect another vessel until we are sure we know what the other vessel is doing. It is all too easy to make assumptions as to what another vessel is doing, when it is being tracked on the radar, but the only way to be sure of what their true course is, is to plot the relative track of the vessel in relation to the track of our vessel.

Many commercial radars can plot other vessels automatically, using a system called ARPA – Automatic Radar Plotting Aid. Most ARPA systems can plot 25 or more targets, indicating for each one, its true course, speed and the Closest Point of Approach (CPA) to your vessel. Some yacht radars are fitted with a smaller system, termed a Mini-ARPA, that can track perhaps five or six targets, and even the most basic system should be able to give the course, speed and CPA for each target.

For those of us sailing without the benefit of ARPA, we must use other methods for plotting.

The most basic way to mark a target on the radar screen is to put the Electronic Bearing Line (the EBL) and the Variable Range Marker onto the target, and watch to see what happens. If the radar is not compass stabilised, then we must hold a steady course while watching the other target.

If, as the target approaches, it moves off the EBL, then it probably indicates that we are not on a collision course – the bearing is changing. (Fig. 1)

If the approaching target stays on the EBL, which indicates that the bearing is constant, then we can assume that we are on a collision course. Using the radar in this way provides no further information. It does not tell us what course the other vessel is steering, nor can we determine how close to it we will come.

A slightly more sophisticated approach would be to mark the position of the target at regular intervals, perhaps by using a wax pencil directly on the screen of the radar. Once again, if the radar is not compass stabilised, then we must hold a very steady course if the results are to have any meaning at all. After at least three positions have been marked, they can be joined together, and the line extended towards the centre of the screen, to show the relative track of the approaching vessel. We can use the VRM to measure how close this tack comes to our position in the centre of the screen. This will show the Closest Point of Approach of the other vessel. (Fig. 2)

We can even get an idea of the Time of Closest Point of Approach (TCPA). If we note the time of the first and the last observation, we can compare the distance travelled in that time, to the distance remaining to the CPA, and so estimate the TCPA.

This method still does not give us any indication of the actual course of the approaching vessel. In the example, Figure 2, we can see that the approaching vessel will pass close on our starboard side, and we could easily make the assumption that as he approached, we would see his starboard light, and we would be going to pass starboard-to-starboard. However, if we take the trouble to do a proper plot, we will see that that would be a false assumption.

Before the advent of ARPA, the display units of many commercial radars were fitted with transparent concave plastic screens, the so-called reflection plotters. Various targets could be marked on the screen using a wax pencil, and using a flexible ruler, the relative and the true track of each of the targets could be plotted directly on the screen. Since the vast majority of commercial vessels have now

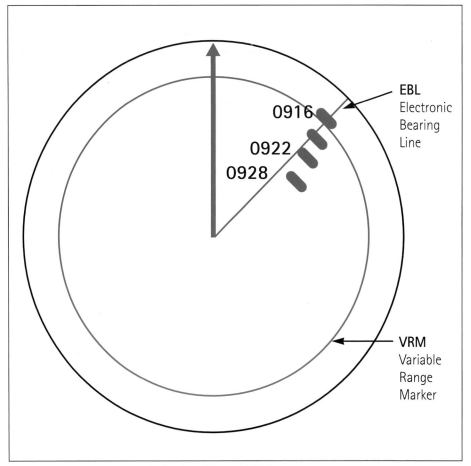

Figure 1. Radar target marked using EBL and VRM.

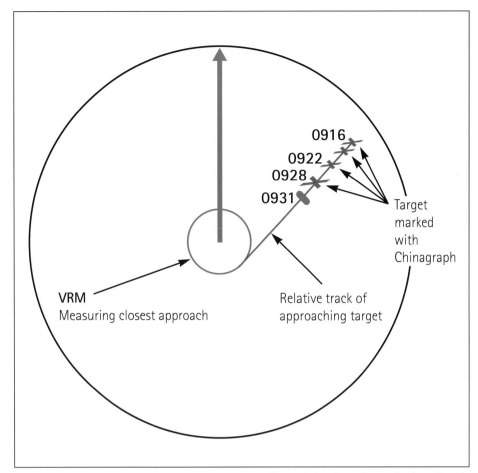

VRM
Measuring closest approach

Relative track of
approaching target

Target
marked
with
Chinagraph

Figure 2. Target is marked using a wax pencil, and the line through the plots is extended to give an indication of the Closest Point of Approach.

been fitted with ARPA, this system has become quite rare. However, the method to construct a plot with a reflection plotter is exactly the same as we are about to look at, for doing a plot on a paper plotting sheet.

A paper plotting sheet is used to represent the screen of the radar display, and usually it will have a scale indicating a 6 mile and a 12 mile range – the two most common ranges used when plotting another vessel. The position of the target is measured as a range and bearing. If the radar is compass stabilised, it would be normal to use the display in the "north up" mode, and using the **E**lectronic **B**earing **L**ine, the compass bearing of the target may be read directly off the screen. If the radar is not compass stabilised, then the bearing read off the screen would be a relative bearing, that is relative to the ship's head.

Although it is possible to do a plot using relative bearings, it would require a steady course to be held throughout the plotting period. If, as is likely, the ship's head swings a degree or two in either direction, then the bearings would be incorrect. If the radar is not compass stabilised, then it is better to note the ship's head at the instant the bearing is taken, and convert the relative bearing of the target to a compass bearing, and do the plot using compass bearings.

For the purposes of the example, we will assume that we are heading due North, at 12.5 knots, and the radar is

compass stabilised, showing a north-up display. The range and bearing of the target is measured, and the position is marked on the plotting sheet. Convention has us label this first point with the letter "O". The time that the position was taken should be noted alongside.

After a suitable period, a second range and bearing of the target is taken, and the position is marked on the chart. We will find that the ensuing mathematics are much easier if we allow 3 minutes or 6 minutes between positions. Once again, the time of the position should be noted alongside. (Fig. 3)

After another similar period, a third range and bearing is taken, and a third position marked on the plotting chart, together with the time. To follow the convention, this last position is labelled as "A". The line O – A is the track of the other vessel relative to us. We must remember that because we are moving at the same time, this line O-A does not indicate the other vessels track nor its heading. However, if we extend the line O-A towards the centre of the plotting sheet, it will show us how close he will come to us, or what is his Closest Point of Approach – his CPA.

By measuring the distance the target has travelled in the time between the plots, and comparing it to the distance to the CPA, it is possible to calculate the Time of **C**losest **P**oint of **A**pproach.

As with the previous example, it is all too easy to assume that we will see the approaching vessel's starboard bow when it gets close enough, but we would be wrong. The line O-A shows the track of the other vessel *relative* to our vessel, which is also moving through the water.

To continue the plot to find the *true* course of the other vessel, we must allow for the motion of our own vessel. To do this, we draw in our course, going <u>towards</u> point O, in this case the line runs from south to north. Then we measure back from point O the distance that we have travelled in the time between plot O and plot A. In this example, since we are doing 12.5 knots, we will have travelled 2.5 miles in 12 minutes. We label this point "W". The line W – O can be remembered as the **W**ay of **O**ur vessel. (Fig. 4)

If we complete the OAW triangle, by joining the points W and A, this line indicates the actual track of the other vessel – it can be remembered as the line W – A showing us

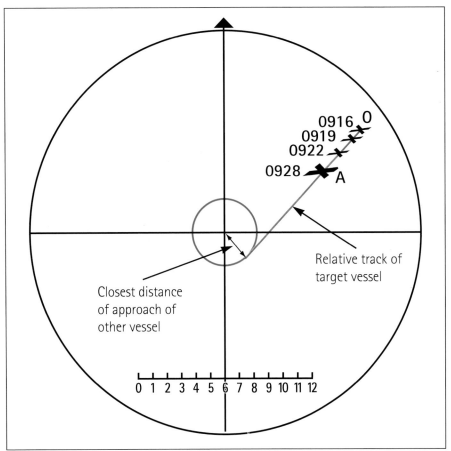

Figure 3. Paper plot of approaching target. The line O – A is extended, to show the Closest point of Approach.

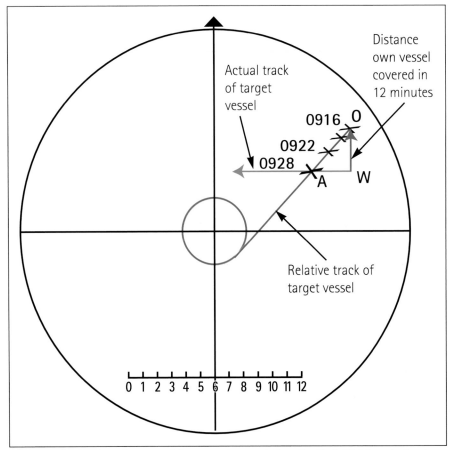

Figure 4. Paper plot of approaching target, completing the O-A-W triangle, to show the true track of the other vessel.

the **W**ay of **A**nother vessel.

Now it can be seen that the other vessel is actually steering due west and should his lights become visible, it will be his port navigation light that we would see, and that we are about to cross his bows, at quite close range. As soon as the plot is done, it becomes readily apparent that we should either slow down, or, better still, make a substantial alteration of course to starboard, to go behind him. If we should we get close enough to see each other, then he will be the stand-on vessel, and we will be obliged to keep out of his way.

With practice, a manual plot like this can be done quite quickly, but to plot more than a couple of vessels at a time gets quite hectic. The skill is to pick the most likely targets, and plot them, to assess the threat, and decide the best course of action.

For those fortunate enough to sail with an ARPA-equipped radar, remember that the relative vectors will indicate the point of closest approach, but will give little idea of the heading of the approaching vessel. It is important to regularly switch to the true vectors, to see the actual heading of the other vessel. This will let you decide which vessel will be the give-way vessel should you get close enough to see each other, and this should help you decide the best action to take.